C-4527 CAREER EXAMINATION SERIES

This is your
PASSBOOK for...

Developmental Disabilities Treatment Team Leader

Test Preparation Study Guide
Questions & Answers

COPYRIGHT NOTICE

This book is SOLELY intended for, is sold ONLY to, and its use is RESTRICTED to individual, bona fide applicants or candidates who qualify by virtue of having seriously filed applications for appropriate license, certificate, professional and/or promotional advancement, higher school matriculation, scholarship, or other legitimate requirements of education and/or governmental authorities.

This book is NOT intended for use, class instruction, tutoring, training, duplication, copying, reprinting, excerption, or adaptation, etc., by:

1) Other publishers
2) Proprietors and/or Instructors of "Coaching" and/or Preparatory Courses
3) Personnel and/or Training Divisions of commercial, industrial, and governmental organizations
4) Schools, colleges, or universities and/or their departments and staffs, including teachers and other personnel
5) Testing Agencies or Bureaus
6) Study groups which seek by the purchase of a single volume to copy and/or duplicate and/or adapt this material for use by the group as a whole without having purchased individual volumes for each of the members of the group
7) Et al.

Such persons would be in violation of appropriate Federal and State statutes.

PROVISION OF LICENSING AGREEMENTS – Recognized educational, commercial, industrial, and governmental institutions and organizations, and others legitimately engaged in educational pursuits, including training, testing, and measurement activities, may address request for a licensing agreement to the copyright owners, who will determine whether, and under what conditions, including fees and charges, the materials in this book may be used them. In other words, a licensing facility exists for the legitimate use of the material in this book on other than an individual basis. However, it is asseverated and affirmed here that the material in this book CANNOT be used without the receipt of the express permission of such a licensing agreement from the Publishers. Inquiries re licensing should be addressed to the company, attention rights and permissions department.

All rights reserved, including the right of reproduction in whole or in part, in any form or by any means, electronic or mechanical, including photocopying, recording, or by any information storage and retrieval system, without permission in writing from the Publisher.

Copyright © 2025 by
National Learning Corporation

212 Michael Drive, Syosset, NY 11791
(516) 921-8888 • www.passbooks.com
E-mail: info@passbooks.com

PASSBOOK® SERIES

THE *PASSBOOK® SERIES* has been created to prepare applicants and candidates for the ultimate academic battlefield – the examination room.

At some time in our lives, each and every one of us may be required to take an examination – for validation, matriculation, admission, qualification, registration, certification, or licensure.

Based on the assumption that every applicant or candidate has met the basic formal educational standards, has taken the required number of courses, and read the necessary texts, the *PASSBOOK® SERIES* furnishes the one special preparation which may assure passing with confidence, instead of failing with insecurity. Examination questions – together with answers – are furnished as the basic vehicle for study so that the mysteries of the examination and its compounding difficulties may be eliminated or diminished by a sure method.

This book is meant to help you pass your examination provided that you qualify and are serious in your objective.

The entire field is reviewed through the huge store of content information which is succinctly presented through a provocative and challenging approach – the question-and-answer method.

A climate of success is established by furnishing the correct answers at the end of each test.

You soon learn to recognize types of questions, forms of questions, and patterns of questioning. You may even begin to anticipate expected outcomes.

You perceive that many questions are repeated or adapted so that you can gain acute insights, which may enable you to score many sure points.

You learn how to confront new questions, or types of questions, and to attack them confidently and work out the correct answers.

You note objectives and emphases, and recognize pitfalls and dangers, so that you may make positive educational adjustments.

Moreover, you are kept fully informed in relation to new concepts, methods, practices, and directions in the field.

You discover that you are actually taking the examination all the time: you are preparing for the examination by "taking" an examination, not by reading extraneous and/or supererogatory textbooks.

In short, this PASSBOOK®, used directedly, should be an important factor in helping you to pass your test.

DEVELOPMENTAL DISABILITIES TREATMENT TEAM LEADER

DUTIES

As a Developmental Disabilities Treatment Team Leader, you would have program and administrative responsibility for the treatment activities of an interdisciplinary treatment team and direct and coordinate a total program tailored to the needs of individuals with intellectual and/or developmental disabilities. You would be responsible for marshaling and assigning team resources to accomplish team goals, and evaluating team programs. You would participate in incident investigations, incident management and reporting, and interaction with the various entities in this regard.

SUBJECT OF EXAMINATION

The written test is designed to test for knowledge, skills, and/or abilities in such areas as:
1. Characteristics and treatment needs of individuals diagnosed with severe intellectual and developmental disabilities;
2. Administrative techniques and practices;
3. Ensuring effective inter/intra agency communications; and
4. Preparing written material.

HOW TO TAKE A TEST

I. YOU MUST PASS AN EXAMINATION

A. WHAT EVERY CANDIDATE SHOULD KNOW

Examination applicants often ask us for help in preparing for the written test. What can I study in advance? What kinds of questions will be asked? How will the test be given? How will the papers be graded?

As an applicant for a civil service examination, you may be wondering about some of these things. Our purpose here is to suggest effective methods of advance study and to describe civil service examinations.

Your chances for success on this examination can be increased if you know how to prepare. Those "pre-examination jitters" can be reduced if you know what to expect. You can even experience an adventure in good citizenship if you know why civil service exams are given.

B. WHY ARE CIVIL SERVICE EXAMINATIONS GIVEN?

Civil service examinations are important to you in two ways. As a citizen, you want public jobs filled by employees who know how to do their work. As a job seeker, you want a fair chance to compete for that job on an equal footing with other candidates. The best-known means of accomplishing this two-fold goal is the competitive examination.

Exams are widely publicized throughout the nation. They may be administered for jobs in federal, state, city, municipal, town or village governments or agencies.

Any citizen may apply, with some limitations, such as the age or residence of applicants. Your experience and education may be reviewed to see whether you meet the requirements for the particular examination. When these requirements exist, they are reasonable and applied consistently to all applicants. Thus, a competitive examination may cause you some uneasiness now, but it is your privilege and safeguard.

C. HOW ARE CIVIL SERVICE EXAMS DEVELOPED?

Examinations are carefully written by trained technicians who are specialists in the field known as "psychological measurement," in consultation with recognized authorities in the field of work that the test will cover. These experts recommend the subject matter areas or skills to be tested; only those knowledges or skills important to your success on the job are included. The most reliable books and source materials available are used as references. Together, the experts and technicians judge the difficulty level of the questions.

Test technicians know how to phrase questions so that the problem is clearly stated. Their ethics do not permit "trick" or "catch" questions. Questions may have been tried out on sample groups, or subjected to statistical analysis, to determine their usefulness.

Written tests are often used in combination with performance tests, ratings of training and experience, and oral interviews. All of these measures combine to form the best-known means of finding the right person for the right job.

II. HOW TO PASS THE WRITTEN TEST

A. NATURE OF THE EXAMINATION

To prepare intelligently for civil service examinations, you should know how they differ from school examinations you have taken. In school you were assigned certain definite pages to read or subjects to cover. The examination questions were quite detailed and usually emphasized memory. Civil service exams, on the other hand, try to discover your present ability to perform the duties of a position, plus your potentiality to learn these duties. In other words, a civil service exam attempts to predict how successful you will be. Questions cover such a broad area that they cannot be as minute and detailed as school exam questions.

In the public service similar kinds of work, or positions, are grouped together in one "class." This process is known as *position-classification*. All the positions in a class are paid according to the salary range for that class. One class title covers all of these positions, and they are all tested by the same examination.

B. FOUR BASIC STEPS

1) Study the announcement

How, then, can you know what subjects to study? Our best answer is: "Learn as much as possible about the class of positions for which you've applied." The exam will test the knowledge, skills and abilities needed to do the work.

Your most valuable source of information about the position you want is the official exam announcement. This announcement lists the training and experience qualifications. Check these standards and apply only if you come reasonably close to meeting them.

The brief description of the position in the examination announcement offers some clues to the subjects which will be tested. Think about the job itself. Review the duties in your mind. Can you perform them, or are there some in which you are rusty? Fill in the blank spots in your preparation.

Many jurisdictions preview the written test in the exam announcement by including a section called "Knowledge and Abilities Required," "Scope of the Examination," or some similar heading. Here you will find out specifically what fields will be tested.

2) Review your own background

Once you learn in general what the position is all about, and what you need to know to do the work, ask yourself which subjects you already know fairly well and which need improvement. You may wonder whether to concentrate on improving your strong areas or on building some background in your fields of weakness. When the announcement has specified "some knowledge" or "considerable knowledge," or has used adjectives like "beginning principles of..." or "advanced ... methods," you can get a clue as to the number and difficulty of questions to be asked in any given field. More questions, and hence broader coverage, would be included for those subjects which are more important in the work. Now weigh your strengths and weaknesses against the job requirements and prepare accordingly.

3) Determine the level of the position

Another way to tell how intensively you should prepare is to understand the level of the job for which you are applying. Is it the entering level? In other words, is this the position in which beginners in a field of work are hired? Or is it an intermediate or advanced level? Sometimes this is indicated by such words as "Junior" or "Senior" in the class title. Other jurisdictions use Roman numerals to designate the level – Clerk I, Clerk II, for example. The word "Supervisor" sometimes appears in the title. If the level is not indicated by the title, check the description of duties. Will you be working under very close supervision, or will you have responsibility for independent decisions in this work?

4) Choose appropriate study materials

Now that you know the subjects to be examined and the relative amount of each subject to be covered, you can choose suitable study materials. For beginning level jobs, or even advanced ones, if you have a pronounced weakness in some aspect of your training, read a modern, standard textbook in that field. Be sure it is up to date and has general coverage. Such books are normally available at your library, and the librarian will be glad to help you locate one. For entry-level positions, questions of appropriate difficulty are chosen – neither highly advanced questions, nor those too simple. Such questions require careful thought but not advanced training.

If the position for which you are applying is technical or advanced, you will read more advanced, specialized material. If you are already familiar with the basic principles of your field, elementary textbooks would waste your time. Concentrate on advanced textbooks and technical periodicals. Think through the concepts and review difficult problems in your field.

These are all general sources. You can get more ideas on your own initiative, following these leads. For example, training manuals and publications of the government agency which employs workers in your field can be useful, particularly for technical and professional positions. A letter or visit to the government department involved may result in more specific study suggestions, and certainly will provide you with a more definite idea of the exact nature of the position you are seeking.

III. KINDS OF TESTS

Tests are used for purposes other than measuring knowledge and ability to perform specified duties. For some positions, it is equally important to test ability to make adjustments to new situations or to profit from training. In others, basic mental abilities not dependent on information are essential. Questions which test these things may not appear as pertinent to the duties of the position as those which test for knowledge and information. Yet they are often highly important parts of a fair examination. For very general questions, it is almost impossible to help you direct your study efforts. What we can do is to point out some of the more common of these general abilities needed in public service positions and describe some typical questions.

1) General information

Broad, general information has been found useful for predicting job success in some kinds of work. This is tested in a variety of ways, from vocabulary lists to questions about current events. Basic background in some field of work, such as sociology or economics, may be sampled in a group of questions. Often these are principles which have become familiar to most persons through exposure rather than through formal training. It is difficult to advise you how to study for these questions; being alert to the world around you is our best suggestion.

2) Verbal ability

An example of an ability needed in many positions is verbal or language ability. Verbal ability is, in brief, the ability to use and understand words. Vocabulary and grammar tests are typical measures of this ability. Reading comprehension or paragraph interpretation questions are common in many kinds of civil service tests. You are given a paragraph of written material and asked to find its central meaning.

3) Numerical ability

Number skills can be tested by the familiar arithmetic problem, by checking paired lists of numbers to see which are alike and which are different, or by interpreting charts and graphs. In the latter test, a graph may be printed in the test booklet which you are asked to use as the basis for answering questions.

4) Observation

A popular test for law-enforcement positions is the observation test. A picture is shown to you for several minutes, then taken away. Questions about the picture test your ability to observe both details and larger elements.

5) Following directions

In many positions in the public service, the employee must be able to carry out written instructions dependably and accurately. You may be given a chart with several columns, each column listing a variety of information. The questions require you to carry out directions involving the information given in the chart.

6) Skills and aptitudes

Performance tests effectively measure some manual skills and aptitudes. When the skill is one in which you are trained, such as typing or shorthand, you can practice. These tests are often very much like those given in business school or high school courses. For many of the other skills and aptitudes, however, no short-time preparation can be made. Skills and abilities natural to you or that you have developed throughout your lifetime are being tested.

Many of the general questions just described provide all the data needed to answer the questions and ask you to use your reasoning ability to find the answers. Your best preparation for these tests, as well as for tests of facts and ideas, is to be at your physical and mental best. You, no doubt, have your own methods of getting into an exam-taking mood and keeping "in shape." The next section lists some ideas on this subject.

IV. KINDS OF QUESTIONS

Only rarely is the "essay" question, which you answer in narrative form, used in civil service tests. Civil service tests are usually of the short-answer type. Full instructions for answering these questions will be given to you at the examination. But in case this is your first experience with short-answer questions and separate answer sheets, here is what you need to know:

1) **Multiple-choice Questions**

Most popular of the short-answer questions is the "multiple choice" or "best answer" question. It can be used, for example, to test for factual knowledge, ability to solve problems or judgment in meeting situations found at work.

A multiple-choice question is normally one of three types—
- It can begin with an incomplete statement followed by several possible endings. You are to find the one ending which *best* completes the statement, although some of the others may not be entirely wrong.
- It can also be a complete statement in the form of a question which is answered by choosing one of the statements listed.

- It can be in the form of a problem – again you select the best answer.

Here is an example of a multiple-choice question with a discussion which should give you some clues as to the method for choosing the right answer:

When an employee has a complaint about his assignment, the action which will *best* help him overcome his difficulty is to
- A. discuss his difficulty with his coworkers
- B. take the problem to the head of the organization
- C. take the problem to the person who gave him the assignment
- D. say nothing to anyone about his complaint

In answering this question, you should study each of the choices to find which is best. Consider choice "A" – Certainly an employee may discuss his complaint with fellow employees, but no change or improvement can result, and the complaint remains unresolved. Choice "B" is a poor choice since the head of the organization probably does not know what assignment you have been given, and taking your problem to him is known as "going over the head" of the supervisor. The supervisor, or person who made the assignment, is the person who can clarify it or correct any injustice. Choice "C" is, therefore, correct. To say nothing, as in choice "D," is unwise. Supervisors have and interest in knowing the problems employees are facing, and the employee is seeking a solution to his problem.

2) True/False Questions

The "true/false" or "right/wrong" form of question is sometimes used. Here a complete statement is given. Your job is to decide whether the statement is right or wrong.

SAMPLE: A roaming cell-phone call to a nearby city costs less than a non-roaming call to a distant city.

This statement is wrong, or false, since roaming calls are more expensive.

This is not a complete list of all possible question forms, although most of the others are variations of these common types. You will always get complete directions for answering questions. Be sure you understand *how* to mark your answers – ask questions until you do.

V. RECORDING YOUR ANSWERS

Computer terminals are used more and more today for many different kinds of exams.

For an examination with very few applicants, you may be told to record your answers in the test booklet itself. Separate answer sheets are much more common. If this separate answer sheet is to be scored by machine – and this is often the case – it is highly important that you mark your answers correctly in order to get credit.

An electronic scoring machine is often used in civil service offices because of the speed with which papers can be scored. Machine-scored answer sheets must be marked with a pencil, which will be given to you. This pencil has a high graphite content which responds to the electronic scoring machine. As a matter of fact, stray dots may register as answers, so do not let your pencil rest on the answer sheet while you are pondering the correct answer. Also, if your pencil lead breaks or is otherwise defective, ask for another.

Since the answer sheet will be dropped in a slot in the scoring machine, be careful not to bend the corners or get the paper crumpled.

The answer sheet normally has five vertical columns of numbers, with 30 numbers to a column. These numbers correspond to the question numbers in your test booklet. After each number, going across the page are four or five pairs of dotted lines. These short dotted lines have small letters or numbers above them. The first two pairs may also have a "T" or "F" above the letters. This indicates that the first two pairs only are to be used if the questions are of the true-false type. If the questions are multiple choice, disregard the "T" and "F" and pay attention only to the small letters or numbers.

Answer your questions in the manner of the sample that follows:

32. The largest city in the United States is
    A. Washington, D.C.
    B. New York City
    C. Chicago
    D. Detroit
    E. San Francisco

1) Choose the answer you think is best. (New York City is the largest, so "B" is correct.)
2) Find the row of dotted lines numbered the same as the question you are answering. (Find row number 32)
3) Find the pair of dotted lines corresponding to the answer. (Find the pair of lines under the mark "B.")
4) Make a solid black mark between the dotted lines.

VI. BEFORE THE TEST

Common sense will help you find procedures to follow to get ready for an examination. Too many of us, however, overlook these sensible measures. Indeed, nervousness and fatigue have been found to be the most serious reasons why applicants fail to do their best on civil service tests. Here is a list of reminders:

- Begin your preparation early – Don't wait until the last minute to go scurrying around for books and materials or to find out what the position is all about.
- Prepare continuously – An hour a night for a week is better than an all-night cram session. This has been definitely established. What is more, a night a week for a month will return better dividends than crowding your study into a shorter period of time.
- Locate the place of the exam – You have been sent a notice telling you when and where to report for the examination. If the location is in a different town or otherwise unfamiliar to you, it would be well to inquire the best route and learn something about the building.
- Relax the night before the test – Allow your mind to rest. Do not study at all that night. Plan some mild recreation or diversion; then go to bed early and get a good night's sleep.
- Get up early enough to make a leisurely trip to the place for the test – This way unforeseen events, traffic snarls, unfamiliar buildings, etc. will not upset you.
- Dress comfortably – A written test is not a fashion show. You will be known by number and not by name, so wear something comfortable.

- Leave excess paraphernalia at home – Shopping bags and odd bundles will get in your way. You need bring only the items mentioned in the official notice you received; usually everything you need is provided. Do not bring reference books to the exam. They will only confuse those last minutes and be taken away from you when in the test room.
- Arrive somewhat ahead of time – If because of transportation schedules you must get there very early, bring a newspaper or magazine to take your mind off yourself while waiting.
- Locate the examination room – When you have found the proper room, you will be directed to the seat or part of the room where you will sit. Sometimes you are given a sheet of instructions to read while you are waiting. Do not fill out any forms until you are told to do so; just read them and be prepared.
- Relax and prepare to listen to the instructions
- If you have any physical problem that may keep you from doing your best, be sure to tell the test administrator. If you are sick or in poor health, you really cannot do your best on the exam. You can come back and take the test some other time.

VII. AT THE TEST

The day of the test is here and you have the test booklet in your hand. The temptation to get going is very strong. Caution! There is more to success than knowing the right answers. You must know how to identify your papers and understand variations in the type of short-answer question used in this particular examination. Follow these suggestions for maximum results from your efforts:

1) Cooperate with the monitor

The test administrator has a duty to create a situation in which you can be as much at ease as possible. He will give instructions, tell you when to begin, check to see that you are marking your answer sheet correctly, and so on. He is not there to guard you, although he will see that your competitors do not take unfair advantage. He wants to help you do your best.

2) Listen to all instructions

Don't jump the gun! Wait until you understand all directions. In most civil service tests you get more time than you need to answer the questions. So don't be in a hurry. Read each word of instructions until you clearly understand the meaning. Study the examples, listen to all announcements and follow directions. Ask questions if you do not understand what to do.

3) Identify your papers

Civil service exams are usually identified by number only. You will be assigned a number; you must not put your name on your test papers. Be sure to copy your number correctly. Since more than one exam may be given, copy your exact examination title.

4) Plan your time

Unless you are told that a test is a "speed" or "rate of work" test, speed itself is usually not important. Time enough to answer all the questions will be provided, but this does not mean that you have all day. An overall time limit has been set. Divide the total time (in minutes) by the number of questions to determine the approximate time you have for each question.

5) Do not linger over difficult questions

If you come across a difficult question, mark it with a paper clip (useful to have along) and come back to it when you have been through the booklet. One caution if you do this – be sure to skip a number on your answer sheet as well. Check often to be sure that you have not lost your place and that you are marking in the row numbered the same as the question you are answering.

6) Read the questions

Be sure you know what the question asks! Many capable people are unsuccessful because they failed to *read* the questions correctly.

7) Answer all questions

Unless you have been instructed that a penalty will be deducted for incorrect answers, it is better to guess than to omit a question.

8) Speed tests

It is often better NOT to guess on speed tests. It has been found that on timed tests people are tempted to spend the last few seconds before time is called in marking answers at random – without even reading them – in the hope of picking up a few extra points. To discourage this practice, the instructions may warn you that your score will be "corrected" for guessing. That is, a penalty will be applied. The incorrect answers will be deducted from the correct ones, or some other penalty formula will be used.

9) Review your answers

If you finish before time is called, go back to the questions you guessed or omitted to give them further thought. Review other answers if you have time.

10) Return your test materials

If you are ready to leave before others have finished or time is called, take ALL your materials to the monitor and leave quietly. Never take any test material with you. The monitor can discover whose papers are not complete, and taking a test booklet may be grounds for disqualification.

VIII. EXAMINATION TECHNIQUES

1) Read the general instructions carefully. These are usually printed on the first page of the exam booklet. As a rule, these instructions refer to the timing of the examination; the fact that you should not start work until the signal and must stop work at a signal, etc. If there are any *special* instructions, such as a choice of questions to be answered, make sure that you note this instruction carefully.

2) When you are ready to start work on the examination, that is as soon as the signal has been given, read the instructions to each question booklet, underline any key words or phrases, such as *least, best, outline, describe* and the like. In this way you will tend to answer as requested rather than discover on reviewing your paper that you *listed without describing*, that you selected the *worst* choice rather than the *best* choice, etc.

3) If the examination is of the objective or multiple-choice type – that is, each question will also give a series of possible answers: A, B, C or D, and you are called upon to select the best answer and write the letter next to that answer on your answer paper – it is advisable to start answering each question in turn. There may be anywhere from 50 to 100 such questions in the three or four hours allotted and you can see how much time would be taken if you read through all the questions before beginning to answer any. Furthermore, if you come across a question or group of questions which you know would be difficult to answer, it would undoubtedly affect your handling of all the other questions.

4) If the examination is of the essay type and contains but a few questions, it is a moot point as to whether you should read all the questions before starting to answer any one. Of course, if you are given a choice – say five out of seven and the like – then it is essential to read all the questions so you can eliminate the two that are most difficult. If, however, you are asked to answer all the questions, there may be danger in trying to answer the easiest one first because you may find that you will spend too much time on it. The best technique is to answer the first question, then proceed to the second, etc.

5) Time your answers. Before the exam begins, write down the time it started, then add the time allowed for the examination and write down the time it must be completed, then divide the time available somewhat as follows:
    - If 3-1/2 hours are allowed, that would be 210 minutes. If you have 80 objective-type questions, that would be an average of 2-1/2 minutes per question. Allow yourself no more than 2 minutes per question, or a total of 160 minutes, which will permit about 50 minutes to review.
    - If for the time allotment of 210 minutes there are 7 essay questions to answer, that would average about 30 minutes a question. Give yourself only 25 minutes per question so that you have about 35 minutes to review.

6) The most important instruction is to *read each question* and make sure you know what is wanted. The second most important instruction is to *time yourself properly* so that you answer every question. The third most important instruction is to *answer every question*. Guess if you have to but include something for each question. Remember that you will receive no credit for a blank and will probably receive some credit if you write something in answer to an essay question. If you guess a letter – say "B" for a multiple-choice question – you may have guessed right. If you leave a blank as an answer to a multiple-choice question, the examiners may respect your feelings but it will not add a point to your score. Some exams may penalize you for wrong answers, so in such cases *only*, you may not want to guess unless you have some basis for your answer.

7) Suggestions
    a. Objective-type questions
        1. Examine the question booklet for proper sequence of pages and questions
        2. Read all instructions carefully
        3. Skip any question which seems too difficult; return to it after all other questions have been answered
        4. Apportion your time properly; do not spend too much time on any single question or group of questions

5. Note and underline key words – *all, most, fewest, least, best, worst, same, opposite,* etc.
6. Pay particular attention to negatives
7. Note unusual option, e.g., unduly long, short, complex, different or similar in content to the body of the question
8. Observe the use of "hedging" words – *probably, may, most likely,* etc.
9. Make sure that your answer is put next to the same number as the question
10. Do not second-guess unless you have good reason to believe the second answer is definitely more correct
11. Cross out original answer if you decide another answer is more accurate; do not erase until you are ready to hand your paper in
12. Answer all questions; guess unless instructed otherwise
13. Leave time for review

   b. Essay questions
   1. Read each question carefully
   2. Determine exactly what is wanted. Underline key words or phrases.
   3. Decide on outline or paragraph answer
   4. Include many different points and elements unless asked to develop any one or two points or elements
   5. Show impartiality by giving pros and cons unless directed to select one side only
   6. Make and write down any assumptions you find necessary to answer the questions
   7. Watch your English, grammar, punctuation and choice of words
   8. Time your answers; don't crowd material

8) Answering the essay question

Most essay questions can be answered by framing the specific response around several key words or ideas. Here are a few such key words or ideas:

M's: manpower, materials, methods, money, management
P's: purpose, program, policy, plan, procedure, practice, problems, pitfalls, personnel, public relations

   a. Six basic steps in handling problems:
   1. Preliminary plan and background development
   2. Collect information, data and facts
   3. Analyze and interpret information, data and facts
   4. Analyze and develop solutions as well as make recommendations
   5. Prepare report and sell recommendations
   6. Install recommendations and follow up effectiveness

   b. Pitfalls to avoid
   1. *Taking things for granted* – A statement of the situation does not necessarily imply that each of the elements is necessarily true; for example, a complaint may be invalid and biased so that all that can be taken for granted is that a complaint has been registered

2. *Considering only one side of a situation* – Wherever possible, indicate several alternatives and then point out the reasons you selected the best one
3. *Failing to indicate follow up* – Whenever your answer indicates action on your part, make certain that you will take proper follow-up action to see how successful your recommendations, procedures or actions turn out to be
4. *Taking too long in answering any single question* – Remember to time your answers properly

IX. AFTER THE TEST

Scoring procedures differ in detail among civil service jurisdictions although the general principles are the same. Whether the papers are hand-scored or graded by machine we have described, they are nearly always graded by number. That is, the person who marks the paper knows only the number – never the name – of the applicant. Not until all the papers have been graded will they be matched with names. If other tests, such as training and experience or oral interview ratings have been given, scores will be combined. Different parts of the examination usually have different weights. For example, the written test might count 60 percent of the final grade, and a rating of training and experience 40 percent. In many jurisdictions, veterans will have a certain number of points added to their grades.

After the final grade has been determined, the names are placed in grade order and an eligible list is established. There are various methods for resolving ties between those who get the same final grade – probably the most common is to place first the name of the person whose application was received first. Job offers are made from the eligible list in the order the names appear on it. You will be notified of your grade and your rank as soon as all these computations have been made. This will be done as rapidly as possible.

People who are found to meet the requirements in the announcement are called "eligibles." Their names are put on a list of eligible candidates. An eligible's chances of getting a job depend on how high he stands on this list and how fast agencies are filling jobs from the list.

When a job is to be filled from a list of eligibles, the agency asks for the names of people on the list of eligibles for that job. When the civil service commission receives this request, it sends to the agency the names of the three people highest on this list. Or, if the job to be filled has specialized requirements, the office sends the agency the names of the top three persons who meet these requirements from the general list.

The appointing officer makes a choice from among the three people whose names were sent to him. If the selected person accepts the appointment, the names of the others are put back on the list to be considered for future openings.

That is the rule in hiring from all kinds of eligible lists, whether they are for typist, carpenter, chemist, or something else. For every vacancy, the appointing officer has his choice of any one of the top three eligibles on the list. This explains why the person whose name is on top of the list sometimes does not get an appointment when some of the persons lower on the list do. If the appointing officer chooses the second or third eligible, the No. 1 eligible does not get a job at once, but stays on the list until he is appointed or the list is terminated.

X. HOW TO PASS THE INTERVIEW TEST

The examination for which you applied requires an oral interview test. You have already taken the written test and you are now being called for the interview test – the final part of the formal examination.

You may think that it is not possible to prepare for an interview test and that there are no procedures to follow during an interview. Our purpose is to point out some things you can do in advance that will help you and some good rules to follow and pitfalls to avoid while you are being interviewed.

What is an interview supposed to test?

The written examination is designed to test the technical knowledge and competence of the candidate; the oral is designed to evaluate intangible qualities, not readily measured otherwise, and to establish a list showing the relative fitness of each candidate – as measured against his competitors – for the position sought. Scoring is not on the basis of "right" and "wrong," but on a sliding scale of values ranging from "not passable" to "outstanding." As a matter of fact, it is possible to achieve a relatively low score without a single "incorrect" answer because of evident weakness in the qualities being measured.

Occasionally, an examination may consist entirely of an oral test – either an individual or a group oral. In such cases, information is sought concerning the technical knowledges and abilities of the candidate, since there has been no written examination for this purpose. More commonly, however, an oral test is used to supplement a written examination.

Who conducts interviews?

The composition of oral boards varies among different jurisdictions. In nearly all, a representative of the personnel department serves as chairman. One of the members of the board may be a representative of the department in which the candidate would work. In some cases, "outside experts" are used, and, frequently, a businessman or some other representative of the general public is asked to serve. Labor and management or other special groups may be represented. The aim is to secure the services of experts in the appropriate field.

However the board is composed, it is a good idea (and not at all improper or unethical) to ascertain in advance of the interview who the members are and what groups they represent. When you are introduced to them, you will have some idea of their backgrounds and interests, and at least you will not stutter and stammer over their names.

What should be done before the interview?

While knowledge about the board members is useful and takes some of the surprise element out of the interview, there is other preparation which is more substantive. It *is* possible to prepare for an oral interview – in several ways:

1) Keep a copy of your application and review it carefully before the interview

This may be the only document before the oral board, and the starting point of the interview. Know what education and experience you have listed there, and the sequence and dates of all of it. Sometimes the board will ask you to review the highlights of your experience for them; you should not have to hem and haw doing it.

2) Study the class specification and the examination announcement

Usually, the oral board has one or both of these to guide them. The qualities, characteristics or knowledges required by the position sought are stated in these documents. They offer valuable clues as to the nature of the oral interview. For example, if the job involves supervisory responsibilities, the announcement will usually indicate that knowledge of modern supervisory methods and the qualifications of the candidate as a supervisor will be tested. If so, you can expect such questions, frequently in the form of a hypothetical situation which you are expected to solve. NEVER go into an oral without knowledge of the duties and responsibilities of the job you seek.

3) Think through each qualification required

Try to visualize the kind of questions you would ask if you were a board member. How well could you answer them? Try especially to appraise your own knowledge and background in each area, *measured against the job sought*, and identify any areas in which you are weak. Be critical and realistic – do not flatter yourself.

4) Do some general reading in areas in which you feel you may be weak

For example, if the job involves supervision and your past experience has NOT, some general reading in supervisory methods and practices, particularly in the field of human relations, might be useful. Do NOT study agency procedures or detailed manuals. The oral board will be testing your understanding and capacity, not your memory.

5) Get a good night's sleep and watch your general health and mental attitude

You will want a clear head at the interview. Take care of a cold or any other minor ailment, and of course, no hangovers.

What should be done on the day of the interview?

Now comes the day of the interview itself. Give yourself plenty of time to get there. Plan to arrive somewhat ahead of the scheduled time, particularly if your appointment is in the fore part of the day. If a previous candidate fails to appear, the board might be ready for you a bit early. By early afternoon an oral board is almost invariably behind schedule if there are many candidates, and you may have to wait. Take along a book or magazine to read, or your application to review, but leave any extraneous material in the waiting room when you go in for your interview. In any event, relax and compose yourself.

The matter of dress is important. The board is forming impressions about you – from your experience, your manners, your attitude, and your appearance. Give your personal appearance careful attention. Dress your best, but not your flashiest. Choose conservative, appropriate clothing, and be sure it is immaculate. This is a business interview, and your appearance should indicate that you regard it as such. Besides, being well groomed and properly dressed will help boost your confidence.

Sooner or later, someone will call your name and escort you into the interview room. *This is it.* From here on you are on your own. It is too late for any more preparation. But remember, you asked for this opportunity to prove your fitness, and you are here because your request was granted.

What happens when you go in?

The usual sequence of events will be as follows: The clerk (who is often the board stenographer) will introduce you to the chairman of the oral board, who will introduce you to the other members of the board. Acknowledge the introductions before you sit down. Do not be surprised if you find a microphone facing you or a stenotypist sitting by. Oral interviews are usually recorded in the event of an appeal or other review.

Usually the chairman of the board will open the interview by reviewing the highlights of your education and work experience from your application – primarily for the benefit of the other members of the board, as well as to get the material into the record. Do not interrupt or comment unless there is an error or significant misinterpretation; if that is the case, do not hesitate. But do not quibble about insignificant matters. Also, he will usually ask you some question about your education, experience or your present job – partly to get you to start talking and to establish the interviewing "rapport." He may start the actual questioning, or turn it over to one of the other members. Frequently, each member undertakes the questioning on a particular area, one in which he is perhaps most competent, so you can expect each member to participate in the examination. Because time is limited, you may also expect some rather abrupt switches in the direction the questioning takes, so do not be upset by it. Normally, a board member will not pursue a single line of questioning unless he discovers a particular strength or weakness.

After each member has participated, the chairman will usually ask whether any member has any further questions, then will ask you if you have anything you wish to add. Unless you are expecting this question, it may floor you. Worse, it may start you off on an extended, extemporaneous speech. The board is not usually seeking more information. The question is principally to offer you a last opportunity to present further qualifications or to indicate that you have nothing to add. So, if you feel that a significant qualification or characteristic has been overlooked, it is proper to point it out in a sentence or so. Do not compliment the board on the thoroughness of their examination – they have been sketchy, and you know it. If you wish, merely say, "No thank you, I have nothing further to add." This is a point where you can "talk yourself out" of a good impression or fail to present an important bit of information. Remember, *you close the interview yourself.*

The chairman will then say, "That is all, Mr. _____, thank you." Do not be startled; the interview is over, and quicker than you think. Thank him, gather your belongings and take your leave. Save your sigh of relief for the other side of the door.

How to put your best foot forward

Throughout this entire process, you may feel that the board individually and collectively is trying to pierce your defenses, seek out your hidden weaknesses and embarrass and confuse you. Actually, this is not true. They are obliged to make an appraisal of your qualifications for the job you are seeking, and they want to see you in your best light. Remember, they must interview all candidates and a non-cooperative candidate may become a failure in spite of their best efforts to bring out his qualifications. Here are 15 suggestions that will help you:

1) Be natural – Keep your attitude confident, not cocky

If you are not confident that you can do the job, do not expect the board to be. Do not apologize for your weaknesses, try to bring out your strong points. The board is interested in a positive, not negative, presentation. Cockiness will antagonize any board member and make him wonder if you are covering up a weakness by a false show of strength.

2) Get comfortable, but don't lounge or sprawl

Sit erectly but not stiffly. A careless posture may lead the board to conclude that you are careless in other things, or at least that you are not impressed by the importance of the occasion. Either conclusion is natural, even if incorrect. Do not fuss with your clothing, a pencil or an ashtray. Your hands may occasionally be useful to emphasize a point; do not let them become a point of distraction.

3) Do not wisecrack or make small talk

This is a serious situation, and your attitude should show that you consider it as such. Further, the time of the board is limited – they do not want to waste it, and neither should you.

4) Do not exaggerate your experience or abilities

In the first place, from information in the application or other interviews and sources, the board may know more about you than you think. Secondly, you probably will not get away with it. An experienced board is rather adept at spotting such a situation, so do not take the chance.

5) If you know a board member, do not make a point of it, yet do not hide it

Certainly you are not fooling him, and probably not the other members of the board. Do not try to take advantage of your acquaintanceship – it will probably do you little good.

6) Do not dominate the interview

Let the board do that. They will give you the clues – do not assume that you have to do all the talking. Realize that the board has a number of questions to ask you, and do not try to take up all the interview time by showing off your extensive knowledge of the answer to the first one.

7) Be attentive

You only have 20 minutes or so, and you should keep your attention at its sharpest throughout. When a member is addressing a problem or question to you, give him your undivided attention. Address your reply principally to him, but do not exclude the other board members.

8) Do not interrupt

A board member may be stating a problem for you to analyze. He will ask you a question when the time comes. Let him state the problem, and wait for the question.

9) Make sure you understand the question

Do not try to answer until you are sure what the question is. If it is not clear, restate it in your own words or ask the board member to clarify it for you. However, do not haggle about minor elements.

10) Reply promptly but not hastily

A common entry on oral board rating sheets is "candidate responded readily," or "candidate hesitated in replies." Respond as promptly and quickly as you can, but do not jump to a hasty, ill-considered answer.

11) Do not be peremptory in your answers

A brief answer is proper – but do not fire your answer back. That is a losing game from your point of view. The board member can probably ask questions much faster than you can answer them.

12) Do not try to create the answer you think the board member wants

He is interested in what kind of mind you have and how it works – not in playing games. Furthermore, he can usually spot this practice and will actually grade you down on it.

13) Do not switch sides in your reply merely to agree with a board member

Frequently, a member will take a contrary position merely to draw you out and to see if you are willing and able to defend your point of view. Do not start a debate, yet do not surrender a good position. If a position is worth taking, it is worth defending.

14) Do not be afraid to admit an error in judgment if you are shown to be wrong

The board knows that you are forced to reply without any opportunity for careful consideration. Your answer may be demonstrably wrong. If so, admit it and get on with the interview.

15) Do not dwell at length on your present job

The opening question may relate to your present assignment. Answer the question but do not go into an extended discussion. You are being examined for a *new* job, not your present one. As a matter of fact, try to phrase ALL your answers in terms of the job for which you are being examined.

Basis of Rating

Probably you will forget most of these "do's" and "don'ts" when you walk into the oral interview room. Even remembering them all will not ensure you a passing grade. Perhaps you did not have the qualifications in the first place. But remembering them will help you to put your best foot forward, without treading on the toes of the board members.

Rumor and popular opinion to the contrary notwithstanding, an oral board wants you to make the best appearance possible. They know you are under pressure – but they also want to see how you respond to it as a guide to what your reaction would be under the pressures of the job you seek. They will be influenced by the degree of poise you display, the personal traits you show and the manner in which you respond.

ABOUT THIS BOOK

This book contains tests divided into Examination Sections. Go through each test, answering every question in the margin. We have also attached a sample answer sheet at the back of the book that can be removed and used. At the end of each test look at the answer key and check your answers. On the ones you got wrong, look at the right answer choice and learn. Do not fill in the answers first. Do not memorize the questions and answers, but understand the answer and principles involved. On your test, the questions will likely be different from the samples. Questions are changed and new ones added. If you understand these past questions you should have success with any changes that arise. Tests may consist of several types of questions. We have additional books on each subject should more study be advisable or necessary for you. Finally, the more you study, the better prepared you will be. This book is intended to be the last thing you study before you walk into the examination room. Prior study of relevant texts is also recommended. NLC publishes some of these in our Fundamental Series. Knowledge and good sense are important factors in passing your exam. Good luck also helps. So now study this Passbook, absorb the material contained within and take that knowledge into the examination. Then do your best to pass that exam.

EXAMINATION SECTION

EXAMINATION SECTION
TEST 1

DIRECTIONS: Each question or incomplete statement is followed by several suggested answers or completions. Select the one that BEST answers the question or completes the statement. *PRINT THE LETTER OF THE CORRECT ANSWER IN THE SPACE AT THE RIGHT*

1. Which of the following statements is TRUE?

    A. The goal of normalization is to allow one to do whatever one likes.
    B. Normalization involves making a person become normal.
    C. Normalization advocates that whenever possible, people's perceptions of developmentally disabled individuals must be enhanced or improved.
    D. Normalization advocates encouraging the developmentally disabled to be just like everyone else.

2. It is important to view the developmentally disabled as

    A. helpless
    B. unable to make decisions
    C. deviant
    D. none of the above

3. All of the following would be considered good practice EXCEPT

    A. providing residential services in the community, rather than in an isolated area
    B. placing residential homes next to rural prisons
    C. providing access in residences to accommodate those who are non-ambulatory
    D. avoiding excessive rules that tend to separate staff from residents

4. All of the following are true in normalization EXCEPT

    A. family involvement in normalization is usually not helpful to achieving the goal
    B. clients should be involved, when possible, in selecting programming in order to develop independence
    C. program options should emphasize autonomy, independence, integration, and productivity
    D. it is a good idea when possible to have day programming located apart from the living setting

5. Benefits of normalization include all of the following EXCEPT

    A. development of self-confidence and self-esteem in the developmentally disabled
    B. social integration of the developmentally disabled
    C. positive changes in societal attitudes regarding the developmentally disabled
    D. societal acceptance of deviance

6. All of the following statements are true EXCEPT:

    A. Normalization means that normal conditions of life should be made available to developmentally disabled people
    B. Attitudes toward the mentally disabled have a great effect on the way they are treated, and, consequently, on their chances for living a productive, normal life

C. It is highly unlikely that efforts at normalization will succeed in most communities
D. What is normal or typical in one society may not be normal or typical in another

7. In normalization, the means used to teach a skill are as important as the skill itself.
In teaching adults, which of the following would be MOST appropriate?

   A. Working individually with someone after dinner in order to teach him or her how to brush their teeth
   B. Teaching pouring skills with sand in a sandbox
   C. Teaching how to button clothes by using a doll for practice
   D. Teaching how to tie shoelaces by first working With a baby shoe

8. Which of the following statements is TRUE?

   A. Residents' chore duties in a community residence should only change three times a year.
   B. Entrance into a community residence should be solely determined by an individual's need for a place to live.
   C. Using a task analysis for a client would involve breaking down a complex task into smaller, more understandable parts.
   D. Clients should be allowed to eat when and what they choose.

9. Select the one statement below that is NOT true of supervised community residences.
A supervised community residence

   A. can provide short-term residence for individuals who need only training and experience in activities of daily living after a period of institutionalization or as an alternative to institutionalization
   B. can provide an institutional setting for those people who need it
   C. can provide long-term residence for individuals who are unlikely to acquire the skills necessary for more independent living
   D. usually requires staff on site at all times

10. All of the following are goals of community residences EXCEPT

    A. providing a home environment for developmentally disabled persons
    B. providing a setting where clients can learn the skills necessary to live in the least restrictive environment
    C. providing a setting where the developmentally disabled can acquire the skills necessary to live as independently as possible
    D. the community residence allows for the maximum level of independence inconsistent with a person's disability and functional level

11. All of the following statements are true EXCEPT:

    A. A community residence does not need to adhere to the principle of normalization in its physical or social structure
    B. The term least restrictive environment refers to an environment which most resembles that of non-handicapped peers where the needs of developmentally disabled persons can be met

C. A person's length of stay in a community residence extends only until a person has attained the skills and motivation to function successfully in a less restrictive setting
D. The purposes of a community residence may vary so that people with different ranges of abilities and levels of functioning may be served

12. All of the following statements are true EXCEPT:

    A. Developmentally disabled persons residing in community residences must be afforded privacy, personal space, and freedom of access to the house as is consistent with their age and program needs
    B. Transportation should be available from the nearest institution so that people in community residences have access to the community
    C. The service needs of each person in a community residence should be individually planned by an interdisciplinary team
    D. An interdisciplinary team should include staff of the community residence, providers of program and support services, and, if appropriate, the developmentally disabled person's correspondent

13. All of the following statements are true EXCEPT:

    A. Supportive community residences are not required to provide staff on site 24 hours a day
    B. Residents in supervised community residences may need more assistance in activities of daily living than persons residing in supportive community residences
    C. An aim of a community residence is to maintain a family and home-like environment
    D. Those living in a community residence shall spend at least three hours per weekday and one evening per week in programs and activities at the residence

14. In working in treatment teams, it is MOST important for team members to

    A. communicate effectively with each other
    B. keep morale high
    C. attend meetings on time
    D. enjoy working with each other

15. All of the following statements are true EXCEPT:

    A. In teaching self-care skills, many tasks may need to be divided into sub-parts
    B. Tasks which are easiest to learn should generally be taught first
    C. Changes in routine are very helpful when teaching the developmentally disabled a new skill
    D. The severely disabled do not learn as well from verbal instruction as they do from demonstration of a skill

16. All of the following statements are true EXCEPT:

    A. It is important to evaluate the client's readiness to attempt learning a particular task before starting to teach the task
    B. It is better to do a task for a client if the task may take much time and effort on his or her part
    C. People generally learn faster when their efforts lead to an enjoyable activity
    D. It is best when teaching a certain skill to begin with a small group when possible

17. All of the following statements are true EXCEPT:
    A. The expectations of a staff person of how well a client will be able to perform a certain task can influence daily living skills
    B. Environmental factors can influence daily living skills
    C. After seeing a skill demonstrated, a client should practice the skill
    D. A client will make a greater effort if he or she feels ill at ease with the instructor, and knows the instructor will become impatient if he or she continues to make mistakes

18. Of the following, the BEST way to teach a client an activity of daily living is to
    A. describe the steps to the client
    B. read the directions to the client
    C. break the activity into steps and have the client learn one step at a time
    D. have a client who can perform the task teach the client who cannot

19. All of the following are important steps in teaching a living skill EXCEPT
    A. defining the skill clearly
    B. determining the size of the skill
    C. breaking down each major step into substeps and sub-substeps as necessary
    D. rewarding the accomplishment of each step with candy

20. When teaching a daily living skill, it is important to keep in mind all of the following EXCEPT
    A. using concrete and specific language
    B. punishment can be a highly effective learning device
    C. matching the size of the skill to the client's ability level
    D. demonstrating what you want the resident to do

KEY (CORRECT ANSWERS)

1.	C		11.	A
2.	D		12.	B
3.	B		13.	D
4.	A		14.	A
5.	D		15.	C
6.	C		16.	B
7.	A		17.	D
8.	C		18.	C
9.	B		19.	D
10.	D		20.	B

TEST 2

DIRECTIONS: Each question or incomplete statement is followed by several suggested answers or completions. Select the one that BEST answers the question or completes the statement. *PRINT THE LETTER OF THE CORRECT ANSWER IN THE SPACE AT THE RIGHT.*

1. All of the following would be considered qualities of a developmental disability EXCEPT the disability

    A. may be attributable to autism
    B. has continued or can be expected to continue indefinitely
    C. can be easily overcome
    D. may be attributable to cerebral palsy or neurological impairment

2. The condition of autism

    A. applies to those people who have little or no control over their motor skills
    B. is hereditary
    C. is characterized by severe disorders of communication and behavior
    D. begins most frequently in adulthood

3. Secondary childhood autism differs from primary childhood autism in that

    A. primary childhood autism is more difficult to treat
    B. secondary childhood autism is secondary to disturbances such as brain damage
    C. secondary childhood autism is not as severe a disorder
    D. secondary childhood autism is less likely to interfere with behavior patterns

4. Which of the following would be LEAST adversely affected by autism?

    A. Interpersonal relations
    B. Learning
    C. Developmental rate and sequences
    D. Motor skills

5. Which of the following statements is NOT true?

    A. Cerebral palsy refers to a condition resulting from damage to the brain that may occur before, during or after birth and results in the loss of control over voluntary muscles in the body.
    B. Ataxic cerebral palsy is characterized by an inability to maintain normal balance.
    C. Someone with athetoid cerebral palsy would find it easier to maintain purposefulness of movements than someone with spastic cerebral palsy.
    D. Mixed cerebral palsy refers to the combination of two or more of the following categories of cerebral palsy such as the spastic, athetoid, ataxic, tremor, and rigid types.

6. All of the following are true about epilepsy EXCEPT

    A. epilepsy does not usually involve a loss of consciousness
    B. an *aura* often appears to the individual before a *grand mal* seizure occurs

C. people experiencing *petit mal* seizures are seldom aware that a seizure has occurred
D. status epilepticus, psychomotor, and Jacksonian are all forms of epilepsy

7. All of the following statements are true of developmental disability EXCEPT:

    A. The prevalence in the general total population is less than 3% of the population
    B. Approximately 89% of the disabled population is mildly disabled
    C. School-age children who are mildly disabled can usually acquire practical skills and useful reading and arithmetic skills
    D. Adults who are mildly disabled cannot usually achieve social and vocational skills adequate for minimum self-support

8. Which of the following statements is NOT true of intellectual disability?

    A. Approximately 6% of the disabled population has an I.Q. of 36-51, 3.5% of the population has an I.Q. of 20-35, and 1.5% of this population has an I.Q. of 19 and below.
    B. A severely disabled person could never achieve limited self-care.
    C. Moderately disabled adults may achieve self-maintenance in unskilled work or semi-skilled work under sheltered conditions.
    D. Severely disabled children can profit from systematic skills training.

9. All of the following refer to neurological impairment EXCEPT

    A. childhood aphasia is a condition characterized by the failure to develop, or difficulty in using, language and speech
    B. epilepsy
    C. minimal brain dysfunction is associated with deviations of the central nervous system
    D. neurological impairment refers to a group of disorders of the central nervous system characterized by dysfunction in one or more, but not all, skills affecting communicative, perceptual, cognitive, memory, attentional, motor control, and appropriate social behaviors

10. Which of the following statements is TRUE?

    A. Autistic children are below average in intelligence level.
    B. All cerebral palsied persons are developmentally disabled.
    C. Once an epileptic seizure has started, it cannot be stopped.
    D. Autism is due to faulty early interactional patterns between child and mother.

11. All of the following are false EXCEPT

    A. recent investigations have found that parents of autistic children have no specific common personality traits and no unusual environmental stresses
    B. cerebral palsied persons cannot understand directions
    C. it is not true that unless controlled seizures can cause further brain damage
    D. the majority of the developmentally disabled are in institutions

10. In serving the needs of autistic persons, the one of the following which is usually LEAST important is the need

    A. for training in social skills
    B. for language stimulation
    C. to deal with potentially self-injurious, repetitive, and aggressive behaviors
    D. to teach skills that would improve intelligence

11. In serving the needs of persons with cerebral palsy, the one of the following which is usually LEAST important is the need

    A. to experience normal movement and sensations as much as possible
    B. to develop fundamental movement patterns which the person can regulate
    C. for experience and guidance in social settings
    D. to restrict their environment

12. All of the following statements are true EXCEPT:

    A. It is important that epileptic persons have balanced diets
    B. Pica, a craving for unnatural food, occurs with all developmentally disabled persons
    C. It has been projected that 50% of those individuals who have cerebral palsy are also developmentally disabled
    D. When working with the developmentally disabled, it is important to encourage sensory-motor stimulation, physical stimulation, language stimulation, social skills training, and the performance of daily living skills

13. When working with neurologically impaired persons, all of the following are true EXCEPT:

    A. There is usually a need for perceptual training
    B. It is important to keep in mind that an individual may know something one day and not know it the next
    C. It may be necessary to remove distracting stimuli
    D. It is important to keep in mind that neurologically impaired persons usually have substantially lower I.Q.'s than the average person

14. The developmentally disabled do NOT have the right to

    A. register and vote in elections
    B. marry
    C. confidentiality of records
    D. hit someone who teases them

15. Which of the following statements is TRUE?

    A. It is important for staff members not to make all of the choices for their developmentally disabled clients.
    B. Distraction is not a good technique to use when trying to channel potentially violent or destructive behavior to a socially acceptable outlet.
    C. Severely and profoundly disabled children do not appear to have a strong need for personal contact.
    D. It is primarily the mildly or moderately disabled child that exhibits the behavior usually associated with developmental disability.

16. All of the following are causes of developmental disability EXCEPT

    A. organic defects
    B. brain lesions
    C. increased sexual activity
    D. chromosomal abnormalities

17. A developmentally disabled patient who is *acting out*

    A. may be trying to communicate that he or she is physically uncomfortable or needs something
    B. should be ignored
    C. should be severely punished
    D. feels comfortable in his or her surroundings

18. In working with the developmentally disabled, all of the following would be appropriate EXCEPT

    A. remembering that seemingly small things, both positive and negative, can be very important to the client
    B. allowing choices whenever possible
    C. maintaining a calm, level-headed attitude during an anxiety-producing situation will reassure clients and help them relax and feel safer
    D. after basic self-help skills have been mastered, it is not necessary to encourage further development

KEY (CORRECT ANSWERS)

1.	C	11.	A
2.	C	12.	D
3.	B	13.	D
4.	D	14.	B
5.	C	15.	D
6.	A	16.	D
7.	D	17.	A
8.	B	18.	C
9.	B	19.	A
10.	C	20.	D

EXAMINATION SECTION
TEST 1

DIRECTIONS: Each question or incomplete statement is followed by several suggested answers or completions. Select the one that BEST answers the question or completes the statement. *PRINT THE LETTER OF THE CORRECT ANSWER IN THE SPACE AT THE RIGHT.*

1. The causes of abnormal behavior include

    A. alcohol and drugs
    B. head injuries and severe infection
    C. diabetes and psychiatric problems
    D. all of the above

1.____

2. All of the following are common reactions to anxiety EXCEPT

    A. depression
    C. denial
    B. flight of ideas
    D. regression

2.____

3. Of the following infections, the one which does NOT produce psychotic syndrome is

    A. chancroid
    C. syphilis
    B. brain abscess
    D. toxoplasmosis

3.____

4. In dealing with emotionally disturbed patients, an EMT should

    A. not assess the patient's needs
    B. intervene in the situation to the extent to which he feels capable
    C. overreact to the patient's behavior or emotional attacks
    D. none of the above

4.____

5. Crisis situations, including periods of _____, may affect the paramedic adversely.

    A. anxiety
    C. impatience
    B. anger
    D. all of the above

5.____

6. A professional attitude MUST be maintained while the paramedic is dealing with emotionally disturbed patients. This attitude can be characterized by all of the following EXCEPT

    A. anger
    C. sensitivity
    B. warmth
    D. compassion

6.____

7. The common emotional difficulties of the paramedic may be managed by

    A. discussing problems and anxieties with co-workers
    B. developing a regular discussion rap session with peers to discuss good and bad experiences
    C. discussing problems with the supervisor
    D. all of the above

7.____

8. There are certain general guidelines for dealing with any patient with a psychiatric problem.
   The one of the following which is NOT among these guidelines is:

   A. Be prepared to spend time with the disturbed patient.
   B. Be as calm and direct as possibl
   C. You do not need to identify yoursel
   D. Assess the patient wherever the emergency occurs.

9. Disorders of motor activity include all of the following EXCEPT

   A. agitation   B. compulsion
   C. perservation   D. restlessness

10. A repetitive action carried out to relieve the anxiety of obsessive thought is called

    A. compulsion   B. delirium
    C. confrontation   D. confabulation

11. The invention of experiences to cover over gaps in memory, seen in patients with certain organic brain syndromes, is

    A. dementia   B. confabulation
    C. psychosis   D. delusion

12. Among the following, which is NOT a symptom of a panic attack?

    A. Shortness of breath or a sensation of being smothered
    B. Feeling of unreality or of stepping apart from oneself
    C. Constant fatigue and no motivation to do anything
    D. Fear of dying and of being crazy

13. Risk factors for violence do NOT include

    A. any place where alcohol is being consumed
    B. natural death in the family
    C. crowd incidents
    D. incidents where violence has already occurred (e.g., shooting, stabbing)

14. Disorders of thinking include all of the following EXCEPT

    A. flight of ideas   B. retardation of thought
    C. compulsions   D. perseveration

15. All of the following are disorders of consciousness EXCEPT

    A. amnesia   B. delirium
    C. fugue stage   D. stupor and coma

16. A repetition of movements that don,t seem to serve any useful purpose is called

    A. compulsion   B. echolalia
    C. stereotyped activity D. all of the above

17. The definition of *compulsion* is:

    A. A repetitive action carried out to relieve the anxiety of obsessive thought
    B. The situation in which a patient cannot sit still
    C. Condition in which the patient echoes the words of the examiner
    D. None of the above

18. The MOST profound disorder of memory is

    A. confabulation
    B. amnesia
    C. illusion
    D. hallucination

19. An acute state of confusion characterized by global impairment of thinking, perception, and memory is called

    A. delusion   B. delirium   C. psychosis   D. dementia

20. Proper pre-hospital management of the manic patient includes

    A. not arguing or getting into a power struggle with the patient
    B. talking to a patient in a quiet place, away from other people
    C. consulting medical command if the patient refuses transport
    D. all of the above

Questions 21-25.

DIRECTIONS: In Questions 21 through 25, match the numbered definition with the lettered disorder, listed in Column I, that it MOST accurately describes. Place the letter of the CORRECT answer in the appropriate space at the right.

COLUMN I
A. Echolalia
B. Illusion
C. Delusion
D. Hallucination
E. Mood

21. Misinterpretation of sensory stimuli

22. False belief

23. Meaningless echoing of the interviewer's words by the patient

24. Sustained and pervasive emotional state

25. Sense of perception not founded on objective reality

KEY (CORRECT ANSWERS)

1. D
2. B
3. A
4. B
5. D

6. A
7. D
8. C
9. C
10. A

11. B
12. C
13. B
14. C
15. A

16. C
17. A
18. B
19. B
20. D

21. B
22. C
23. A
24. E
25. D

TEST 2

DIRECTIONS: Each question or incomplete statement is followed by several suggested answers or completions. Select the one that BEST answers the question or completes the statement. *PRINT THE LETTER OF THE CORRECT ANSWER IN THE SPACE AT THE RIGHT.*

1. The depressed patient can often be readily identified by

    A. a sad expression
    B. bouts of crying
    C. expression of feelings of worthlessness
    D. all of the above

2. The third leading cause of death among the 15- to 25 year-old age group is

    A. diabetes mellitus
    B. rheumatoid arthritis
    C. suicide
    D. congenital heart disease

3. The assessment of every depressed person MUST include an evaluation of

    A. schizophrenia
    B. suicide risk
    C. chronic debilitating illness
    D. anxiety

4. When caring for a patient who is displaying typical stress reactions, you should

    A. act in a calm manner, giving the patient time to gain control of his emotions
    B. quietly and carefully evaluate the situation
    C. stay alert for sudden changes in behavior
    D. all of the above

5. The patient in a psychiatric emergency is far more out of reach and out of control than the person in an emotional emergency.
   In a psychiatric emergency, the patient may do all of the following EXCEPT

    A. try to hurt himself
    B. try to seek help for protection
    C. withdraw, no longer responding to people or to his environment
    D. continue to act depressed, sometimes crying and expressing feelings of worthlessness

6. When a patient is acting as if he may hurt himself or another, you should do all of the following EXCEPT

    A. alert the police
    B. not isolate yourself from your partner or other sources of help
    C. try to restrain the patient by yourself
    D. always be on the watch for weapons

7. A mental disorder characterized by loss of contact with reality is called

    A. psychosis
    B. dementia
    C. phobia
    D. none of the above

8. Anti-psychotic drugs are also called

   A. antidepressants
   B. neuroleptics
   C. anxiolytics
   D. antiepileptics

9. The patient who hears voices commanding him to hurt himself or others must be considered

   A. normal
   B. safe
   C. dangerous
   D. none of the above

10. When in a state of *conversion hysteria,* a person's

    A. reaction may move from extreme anxiety to relative calmness
    B. may transform anxiety to some bodily function
    C. often becomes hysterically blind, deaf, or paralyzed
    D. all of the above

11. Repeating the same idea over and over again is called

    A. perseveration
    B. compulsion
    C. obsession
    D. facilitation

12. _____ is the interviewing technique in which the interviewer encourages the patient to proceed by noncommittal words and gestures.

    A. Echolalia
    B. Facilitation
    C. Affect
    D. None of the above

13. The CHRONIC deterioration of mental function is referred to as

    A. dementia
    B. psychosis
    C. delirium
    D. schizophrenia

14. A persistent idea that a person CANNOT dismiss from his thought is a(n)

    A. affect
    B. obsession
    C. compulsion
    D. delusion

15. An interviewing technique in which the interviewer points out to the patient something of interest in his conversation or behavior is

    A. facilitation
    B. confabulation
    C. confrontation
    D. perseveration

16. It is important for paramedics to be aware of one particular syndrome that may occur in patients taking anti-psychotic medication. This condition is

    A. acute diuresis
    B. acute dystonic reaction
    C. hypertensive crises
    D. none of the above

17. An acute dystonic reaction can be rapidly corrected by

    A. chlorpromazine
    B. prolixin
    C. diphenhydramine
    D. tindal

18. Tranquilizers are also called

   A. neuroleptics B. anxiolytics
   C. chinergics D. stimulants

19. The COMMON symptoms of antipsychotic drugs include

   A. blurred vision B. dry mouth
   C. cardiac dysrhythmias D. all of the above

20. Uncontrolled, disconnected thoughts characterize a disorganized patient who may be

   A. incoherent or rambling in his speech
   B. wandering aimlessly
   C. dressed inappropriately
   D. all of the above

Questions 21-25.

DIRECTIONS: In Questions 21 through 25, match the numbered definition with the lettered disorder, listed in Column I, that it MOST accurately describes. Place the letter of the CORRECT answer in the appropriate space at the right.

COLUMN I
A. Agitation
B. Agoraphobia
C. Flight of ideas
D. Neologism
E. Confabulation

21. Fear of the marketplace

22. An invented word that has meaning only to its inventor

23. The invention of experiences to cover over gaps in memory

24. Extreme restlessness and anxiety

25. Accelerated thinking in which the mind skips very rapidly from one thought to the next

KEY (CORRECT ANSWERS)

1.	D	11.	A
2.	C	12.	B
3.	B	13.	A
4.	D	14.	B
5.	B	15.	C
6.	C	16.	B
7.	A	17.	C
8.	B	18.	B
9.	C	19.	D
10.	D	20.	D

21. B
22. D
23. E
24. A
25. C

EXAMINATION SECTION
TEST 1

DIRECTIONS: Each question or incomplete statement is followed by several suggested answers or completions. Select the one that BEST answers the question or completes the statement. *PRINT THE LETTER OF THE CORRECT ANSWER IN THE SPACE AT THE RIGHT.*

1. A relationship in which a patient becomes dependent on the nurse 1.____

    A. is always unprofessional
    B. is inevitably "bad" for the patient
    C. may be necessary temporarily
    D. impedes learning

2. Anxiety is the CHIEF characteristic of the 2.____

    A. immature personality
    B. psychoneurotic disorder
    C. involutional psychotic reaction
    D. mentally retarded adolescent

3. The mode of psychological adjustment known as regression can BEST be described as 3.____

    A. refusing to think of unpleasant situations
    B. changing to a type of behavior which is characteristic of an earlier period in life
    C. reverting to actions characteristic of an historically early or primitive code of behavior
    D. hostility towards persons or objects that prove frustrating

4. The CHIEF danger in the employment of escape mechanisms as a form of adjustment is that they 4.____

    A. do more harm than good
    B. are socially undesirable
    C. make the experience expensive
    D. leave the basic problem unsolved

5. In essential hypertension, there is a(n) 5.____

    A. *increase* in systolic pressure and a *decrease* in diastolic pressure
    B. *decrease* in systolic pressure and an *increase* in diastolic pressure
    C. *increase* in *both* systolic and diastolic pressure
    D. *decrease* in *both* systolic and diastolic pressure

6. The *initial* paralysis in cerebral vascular accident, regardless of cause, is the type known as 6.____

    A. spastic   B. paraplegic   C. flaccid   D. rigid

7. Cerebral hemorrhage *most frequently* occurs in males in the age range from 7.____

    A. 20 to 30 years   B. 30 to 40 years
    C. 40 to 50 years   D. 50 years and over

17

8. Hereditary progressive muscular dystrophy is a disease characterized by progressive weakness and final atrophy of groups of muscles.
Of the following statements about muscular dystrophy, the one which is LEAST accurate is that

   A. there is no known cure for muscular dystrophy at present
   B. muscular dystrophy is a disease of the central nervous system
   C. early signs of muscular dystrophy are frequent falls, difficulty climbing stairs, development of lordosis, and a waddling gait
   D. therapeutic exercises may have some temporary value in the treatment of muscular dystrophy

9. The home care program is an extension of the hospital's service into the home on an extra-mural basis.
Of the following statements, the one that BEST explains the success of this program is that it

   A. *recognizes* the value to the patient and his family of the preservation of normal family life despite the limitations imposed by the patient's illness
   B. *makes* more hospital beds available for acute illnesses and emergency care
   C. reduces the cost of hospital care by reducing the number of inpatients
   D. *simplifies* hospital administration by reducing the number of chronically ill in hospitals

10. The MOST important of the following reasons for the rehabilitation of the seriously handicapped individual is that

    A. hospitalization of the handicapped is usually prolonged and costly to the community
    B. beds occupied by such patients reduce the number of hospital beds available for acutely ill patients
    C. care of chronically ill or handicapped patients is taxing and difficult for the family, the nurse, and the doctor
    D. it is important to the patient that he be as independent and useful as possible

11. There has been a notable increase in the discharge rate from mental institutions in the state during recent years. This change in statistics may be attributed CHIEFLY to

    A. increasing use of psychoanalysis and better trained personnel
    B. new drugs, changes in admission procedures, and the "open door" policy
    C. the increase in nursing homes for the elderly
    D. the use of psychotherapeutics and early diagnosis of mental illness

12. The PRINCIPAL and BASIC objective of mental hygiene is to

    A. modify attitudes as well as unhealthy behavior secondary to unhealthy attitudes
    B. care for the post-hospitalized psychiatric patient at home
    C. increase mental hygiene clinic services
    D. stimulate interest in improved education for doctors, nurses, and teachers

13. Separation of a child from his own home and placement in a foster home often arouses adverse reactions in the child. Of the following, the one which is MOST serious for the child is

    A. homesickness
    B. withdrawn behavior
    C. rebellion against authority
    D. dislike of new people

14. Behavior problems of the adolescent school child can BEST be explained by the fact that

    A. the adolescent suddenly becomes aware of the opposite sex at this time
    B. the demands made on adolescents by intolerant parents create rebellion against authority
    C. during childhood there is a general disregard of the child's need for independence by parents and other adults
    D. adolescence is a transition period between childhood and adulthood which usually creates feelings of insecurity in the adolescent

15. Of the following, the behavior which is LEAST indicative of serious emotional maladjustment in an adolescent boy is

    A. lying and cheating
    B. shyness and daydreaming
    C. gross overweight
    D. association with a teen-age gang

16. The one of the following diseases which is caused by a birth injury is

    A. cerebral palsy
    B. meningitis
    C. hydrocele
    D. congenital syphilis
    E. epilepsy

17. A delusion is a

    A. disharmony of mind and body
    B. fantastic image formed during sleep
    C. false judgment of objective things
    D. cessation of thought
    E. distorted perception or image

18. The one of the following which is the MOST common form of treatment employed by psychiatrists in treating patients with mental disorders is

    A. hypnotism
    B. hydrotherapy
    C. electroshock
    D. insulin shock
    E. psychotherapy

19. A masochistic person is one who

    A. is very melancholy
    B. has delusions of grandeur about himself
    C. derives pleasure from being cruelly treated
    D. believes in a fatalistic philosophy
    E. derives pleasure from hurting another

20. Surgery is *ESPECIALLY* difficult during the Oedipal period because of the

    A. father attachment
    B. mental age
    C. castration anxieties
    D. rejection complex
    E. separation from siblings

21. A psychometric test is one which attempts to measure

    A. social adjustment
    B. emotional maturity
    C. physical activity
    D. personality development
    E. Intellectual capacity

22. The one of the following conditions which falls into the classification of a psychosis rather than psychoneurosis is

    A. anxiety hysteria
    B. schizophrenia
    C. neurasthenia
    D. convesion hysteria
    E. compulsion neurosis

23. The one of the following which BEST describes psychosomatic medicine is:

    A. The understanding and treatment of both mind and body in illness
    B. The treatment of disease by psychiatric methods only
    C. The separation of mind and body in medical treatment
    D. The psychological testing of all individuals
    E. A system of socialized medical planning

24. The one of the following conditions for which shock treatment is *FREQUENTLY* used is

    A. alcoholism
    B. Parkinson's syndrome
    C. multiple sclerosis
    D. schizophrenia
    E. diabetes

25. The one of the following conditions which is *NOT* caused by the dysfunction of endocrine glands is

    A. myxedema
    B. duodenal ulcer
    C. cretinism
    D. Addison's disease
    E. none of the above

KEY (CORRECT ANSWERS)

1.	C	11.	B
2.	B	12.	A
3.	B	13.	B
4.	D	14.	D
5.	C	15.	D
6.	C	16.	A
7.	D	17.	C
8.	B	18.	E
9.	A	19.	C
10.	D	20.	C

21. E
22. B
23. A
24. D
25. B

TEST 2

DIRECTIONS: Each question or incomplete statement is followed by several suggested answers or completions. Select the one that BEST answers the question or completes the statement. *PRINT THE LETTER OF THE CORRECT ANSWER IN THE SPACE AT THE RIGHT.*

1. Euphoria is a state of

   A. depression B. elation C. ideation D. frustration

2. An ailment found only in older people is

   A. manic depression B. dementia praecox
   C. senile dementia D. tabes dorsalis

3. The permissive policy employed in some mental hospitals is associated with a(n)

   A. increase in assaultive behavior
   B. open door policy
   C. decrease in the use of physical restraint
   D. increase in the use of physical restraint

4. A symptom of dementia praecox is

   A. extroversion B. tic paralysis
   C. unpredictability D. cerebral hemorrhage

5. Substituting an activity in which a person can succeed for one in which he may fail is

   A. sublimation B. projection
   C. rationalization D. compensation

6. Rationalization is the result of

   A. believing what one wants to believe
   B. reflective thinking
   C. scientific thinking
   D. basing conclusions on fact

7. Delusions of persecution are typical of

   A. epilepsy B. regression
   C. schizophrenia D. paranoia

8. A person with an IQ of 85 would be classified as

   A. defective B. normal
   C. dull average D. borderline

9. The term describing physical symptoms that do not arise *ENTIRELY* from physical causes is

   A. organic B. psychoneurotic
   C. psychosomatic D. psychopathological

10. The mechanism of attributing one's own ideas to others is termed

   A. projection
   B. substitution
   C. sublimation
   D. rationalization

11. A child's tendency to pattern after his parents is known as

   A. identification
   B. projection
   C. compensation
   D. substitution

12. Stuttering in children USUALLY originates from

   A. physical handicap
   B. mentally deficient parents
   C. emotional handicap
   D. imitation of other stutterers

13. Acute intoxication may PROPERLY be labeled a psychosis because it involves

   A. intellectual limitations
   B. emotional inadequacies
   C. bodily disease
   D. a severe loss of contact with reality

14. The outstanding change, of the following, in the aging process is that the aged are

   A. irritable
   B. no longer self-reliant
   C. senile
   D. easily influenced by stress

15. Re-adjusting the older person to be somewhat self-sufficient is known as

   A. stabilization
   B. regeneration
   C. rejuvenation
   D. rehabilitation

16. The spastic child usually

   A. is mentally retarded
   B. is potentially schizophrenic
   C. requires speech training
   D. has poor vision

17. Insomnia refers to

   A. unconsciousness
   B. sleeplessness
   C. sleep walking
   D. insensibility

18. A drug recently introduced in the treatment of mental illness is

   A. streptomycin
   B. paramino-salicylic acid
   C. reserpine
   D. cortisone

19. In general, the sleep requirement for an aged person as compared to the sleep requirement for a young adult is

   A. less   B. more   C. the same   D. slightly greater

20. The MOST IMPORTANT aspect of the rehabilitation of a person who has suffered a stroke is the

   A. patient's emotional reaction to self
   B. doctor's attitude toward the patient
   C. nurse's attitude toward the patient
   D. family reaction toward the patient

21. If a patient tells a nurse that he is contemplating committing suicide, the nurse should

   A. not pay any attention, since people who threaten suicide seldom follow through
   B. urge him to consult a psychiatrist, since potential suicides need psychiatric help immediately
   C. be sympathetic. Her sympathy will divert him from his intention
   D. realize that he is a neurotic with whom she will try to work

22. The BEST advice you can give parents disturbed by their five-year-old child's habit of nailbiting is to tell them to

   A. find out what some of the pressures on the child are and try to relieve them
   B. paint the child's fingers with the product "bitter aloes"
   C. point out to the child that this is a baby habit and not desirable in a school child
   D. punish the child by not allowing him to watch television or go to the movies

23. In certain periods of development, anti-social behavior in young children is considered normal. However, of the following situations, the one which merits referral to a mental hygiene clinic is where

   A. a two-year-old persists in hitting his four- year-old brother
   B. a three-year-old develops enuresis when a new baby is brought into the home
   C. a four-year-old runs away from home at every opportunity
   D. a six-year-old is not friendly, has no "pals" after six months in school, and participates in activities only when compelled to

24. Learning occurs

   A. when the child's responses are adequate
   B. when a solution to the situation is obvious
   C. when the adult solves the problems
   D. None of the above

25. The FIRST emotions to become differentiated may be described as

   A. anger and fear
   B. anger and distress
   C. fear and delight
   D. delight and distress

KEY (CORRECT ANSWERS)

1. B
2. C
3. B
4. C
5. D

6. A
7. D
8. C
9. C
10. A

11. A
12. C
13. D
14. D
15. D

16. C
17. B
18. C
19. A
20. A

21. B
22. A
23. D
24. A
25. D

EXAMINATION SECTION
TEST 1

DIRECTIONS: Each question or incomplete statement is followed by several suggested answers or completions. Select the one the BEST answers the question or completes the statement. *PRINT THE LETTER OF THE CORRECT ANSWER IN THE SPACE AT THE RIGHT.*

1. Generally, slow learning is present in about ____% of people who suffer from Duchenne muscular dystrophy.

    A. 30
    B. 50
    C. 70
    D. 90

2. When a particular behavior reliably occurs only in the presence of certain stimulus events, the behavior is said to be

    A. generalized
    B. indiscriminate
    C. internalized
    D. under stimulus control

3. In the placement/training phase of a habilitation program, which of the following actions is associated with the agency's habilitation strategies?

    A. Employing effective prosthetic/accommodation techniques
    B. Gathering longitudinal data on clients
    C. Seeking integrated living arrangements
    D. Updating intersector working arrangements

4. Support and follow-up for transitional employment placements generally lasts for a period of

    A. 30 days
    B. 90 days
    C. 6 months
    D. 1 year

5. In the human brain, functions associated with sensation generally originate in the

    A. cerebellum
    B. septum
    C. occipital lobe
    D. parietal lobe

6. The habilitation specialist's attitude of trust and respect in the presence of a disabled client is known as the

    A. accommodation gesture
    B. protective stance
    C. equity posture
    D. authority position

7. Which of the following is not one of the primary goals noted in the Developmental Disabilities Assistance and Bill of Rights Act?

    A. Symptom alleviation
    B. Community integration
    C. Independence
    D. Productivity

8. The primary advantage associated with the use of functional definitions in relation to service delivery and program design is that these definitions

    A. increase the likelihood that a person with functional limitations will be classified as disabled
    B. simplify administrative tasks such as budgeting and resource allocation
    C. fit in with an established state and federal framework
    D. encourage the individualization of program planning on a person-by-person basis

9. Of the following areas of life activity, in which is a person with epilepsy LEAST likely to experience a deficit?

    A. Cognition
    B. Self-direction
    C. Economic self-sufficiency
    D. Independent living

10. Traditional techniques of behavior modification can be described as each of the following except

    A. dynamic
    B. insight-oriented
    C. systematic
    D. focusing on the past

11. A person's overall life satisfaction is categorized as a(n) _____ quality of life factor.

    A. physical
    B. cognitive
    C. material
    D. social

12. Which of the following behavior treatment techniques is probably LEAST appropriate for affecting changes in the leisure skills of a developmentally disabled client?

    A. Modeling
    B. Response contingent stimulation
    C. Physical prompts
    D. Verbal praise

13. Among developmentally disabled persons, which of the following activities is likely to require the greatest degree of intervention and rehabilitation?

    A. Gross motor control
    B. Housekeeping

C. Eating
D. Grooming

14. Autistic clients can be reliably distinguished from nonautistic disabled clients of similar IQ or mental age on the basis of each of the following, except

    A. cognitive test performance
    B. play patterns
    C. self-care
    D. language features

15. The goals of an individual habilitation plan include socialization, communication, and interaction. Which of the following instructional techniques will be most helpful?

    A. Providing opportunities for decisions and choice
    B. Developing a stimulus-response chain based on task analysis
    C. Teaching generalization of social exchanges to other persons and settings
    D. Presenting multiple training examples within individual sessions

16. Which of the following is a diagnostic condition that is most likely to result in sensory/neurological impairment?

    A. Multiple sclerosis
    B. Hydrocephalus
    C. Epilepsy
    D. Cerebral palsy

17. Which of the following skill domains is relatively strong among clients with spina bifida?

    A. Eye-hand coordination
    B. Mathematics
    C. Abstract reasoning
    D. Expressive language

18. Which of the following statements about generalized reinforcers is false?

    A. Their use takes place in a naturally occurring learning environment.
    B. Satiation is rare due to the wide variety of reinforcers for which they can be exchanged
    C. They bridge the delay between the performance of the behavior and the receipt of additional reinforcers.
    D. They are easy to store and dispense.

19. In the human brain, functions associated with emotions and their expression generally originate in the

    A. parietal lobe
    B. frontal lobe
    C. midbrain
    D. cerebellum

20. When selecting an instructional technique that will be effective with difficult-to-teach clients, it is important to choose the simplest possible successful strategy. The environmental components that need to be addressed include
    I. the possible presence of some behavior that is incompatible with the task being taught
    II. the presence or absence of necessary prerequisite skills
    III. environmental stimuli such as the effectiveness of the instructions
    IV. the motivational system

    A. I and II
    B. II, III and IV
    C. III and IV
    D. I, II, III and IV

21. In the past decade or so, employment services to the disabled have generally changed in each of the following ways, except a(n)

    A. shift to public/private interfacing
    B. shift to separate work facilities for groups of disabled workers
    C. increased need for reportability focusing on person-referenced employment outcome data
    D. increased need for on-site evaluation, training and habitation practices

22. Approximately what percentage of cases of developmental disability have primary biological and medical origins?

    A. 10
    B. 25
    C. 50
    D. 75

23. During play sessions in which a developmentally disabled child is being taught appropriate play behavior, the child's first correct toy-play response after an average of 5 minutes have elapsed is reinforced. This is an example of _____ reinforcement.

    A. variable interval
    B. fixed interval
    C. variable ratio
    D. fixed ratio

24. Three Amendments to the U.S. Constitution have played an essential role in social change as it affects adults with disabilities. Which of the following is not one of them?

    A. Fifth
    B. Eighth
    C. Fourteenth
    D. Sixteenth

25. Overcorrection is a behavior reduction technique that includes the two components of
    A. response cost and modeling
    B. fading and extinction
    C. response cost and differential reinforcement
    D. restitution and positive practice

KEY (CORRECT ANSWERS)

1. C
2. D
3. A
4. C
5. D

6. C
7. A
8. D
9. A
10. C

11. B
12. B
13. B
14. C
15. C

16. C
17. D
18. A
19. C
20. D

21. B
22. B
23. A
24. D
25. D

TEST 2

DIRECTIONS: Each question or incomplete statement is followed by several suggested answers or completions. Select the one the BEST answers the question or completes the statement. *PRINT THE LETTER OF THE CORRECT ANSWER IN THE SPACE AT THE RIGHT.*

1. Which of the following is not an element of behavior analytic pre-vocational and vocational training?

    A. Acquisition, maintenance, and transfer
    B. Individualized training
    C. Qualitative description of behaviors
    D. Repeated assessments

2. According to the Developmental Disabilities Assistance and Bill of Rights Act, which of the following components is/are included in the definition of a severe and chronic "disability"?

    I. It is attributable to a mental or physical impairment, or a combination of both
    II. It reflects the person's need for a combination and sequence of special, interdisciplinary, or generic care, treatment, or other services
    III. It results in substantial functional limitations
    IV. It is attributable to substance dependence or adult-onset mental illness, or a combination of both

    A. I and II
    B. I, II and III
    C. I and IV
    D. I, II, III and IV

3. Which of the following is not a guideline that should be followed in the application of punishment to a developmentally disabled child?

    A. Avoid associating the delivery of punishment with the later delivery of reinforcement
    B. Apply punishment immediately following the behavior
    C. Punishment should be applied in graded steps
    D. . Avoid prolonged or extensive use of punishment

4. Once a trainee has learned a new skill or reduced an inappropriate behavior, habilitation staff should consider the use of a(n)

    A. shaping sequence
    B. descriptive validation
    C. summative assessment
    D. intermittent schedule

5. In the human brain, functions associated with memory and the registration of new information generally originate in the

    A. parietal lobe
    B. temporal lobe

C. frontal lobe
D. hippocampus

6. The nutritional services offered to a person in a community contribute to the ____ of that person's quality of life.

    A. physical
    B. cognitive
    C. material
    D. social

7. The goals of an individual habilitation plan include generalization and mobility across environments. Which of the following instructional techniques will be most helpful?

    A. Determining the appropriate modes of client communication
    B. Sampling a range of relevant stimulus and response variation
    C. Building learning activities on the client's interest
    D. Simplifying the steps involved in a specific behavior

8. When using preference assessments for designing a habilitation program, each of the following is a guideline that should be followed, except

    A. if activities are presented to the person, all should be presented several times in different combinations
    B. program decisions should be made mostly on the basis of the personal interview
    C. each type of assessment should be done over a period of days
    D. equal attention should be paid to duration and quality of interactions

9. A client with muscular dystrophy is having difficulty feeding himself due to weakness in his arms. The first thing that should be tried is to

    A. raise the table or eating surface a bit
    B. fit the client with an elastic cuff that will hold a spoon
    C. feed the client for a while and see if he will attempt to self-feed again
    D. fit the client with special slings that will aid in feeding

10. Which of the following adaptations are most likely to be necessary for developmentally disabled clients who take part in leisure activities?

    A. Personal training
    B. Environmental adaptations
    C. Rule or procedural alterations
    D. Material changes

11. Which of the following is an important consideration when developing a schedule of treatment sessions for an aphasic client?

    A. Aphasia, once corrected, is often followed by a period of dysfluency
    B. Aphasic persons communicate significantly better following periods of rest
    C. The utterings of an aphasic client are usually part of a syndrome
    D. Most aphasia is temporary

12. When a person leans to perform a desired response only in the presence of specific stimulus events, _____ occurred.

    A. generalization
    B. discrimination
    C. habituation
    D. shaping

13. When disabled workers lose their position in an integrated environment, it is usually because they

    A. were never very enthusiastic about the job
    B. have not been able to acquire the necessary skills
    C. did not receive adequate on-the-job support
    D. were unable to deal adequately with interpersonal issues

14. In behavioral modification, a generalized positive reinforcer may be exchanged by a client for a ____ reinforcer.

    A. conditioned
    B. negative
    C. backup
    D. contingent

15. A typical habilitation plan begins with a list of

    A. the client's goals as related to independence and integration
    B. the client's preferences and competencies
    C. a matching of the client with support services
    D. a summary of available resources

16. The primary disadvantage associated with the use of single-step behavior training is that the client

    A. is not aware of the ultimate goal of the behavior
    B. may experience difficulty transferring from skill training to the application session
    C. may not be provided with sufficient opportunities to practice discrimination
    D. does not have the opportunity to learn a skill intensively

17. Clients with ____ spina bifida are most likely to develop scoliosis.

    A. thoracic
    B. mid-lumbar
    C. lower lumbar
    D. sacral

18. Generally speaking, persons with a dual diagnosis are likely to be limited in life activity areas involving

    I. language
    II. independent living
    III. self-direction
    IV. learning

- A. I and IV
- B. II, III and IV
- C. II and III
- D. I, II, III and IV

19. When a client will perform a behavior better if she knows what the final product will be, which of the following instructional strategies is most appropriate?

    A. Forward chaining
    B. Response cost
    C. Backward chaining
    D. Full-sequence training

20. Because of the limited amount of time generally available for behavioral skill instruction, habilitation workers generally make sure that the instruction is guided by each of the following principles, except

    A. strategies should involve action by the client and observation by the instructor
    B. the instruction should focus on functional attributes
    C. improvements brought about by behaviors should all relate to the client's quality of life
    D. the skills taught should relate to the person's life-aim goals

21. When it occurs, a grand mal seizure usually lasts about

    A. 10-15 seconds
    B. 30-60 seconds
    C. 2-5 minutes
    D. 5-7 minutes

22. Which of the following is common to virtually all language training programs for autistic or dual-diagnosis clients?

    A. generalization
    B. teaching in small progressive steps
    C. segregation into phonemes and morphemes
    D. discrimination

23. Affective disorders are categorized as

    A. anxiety disorders
    B. psychoses
    C. syndrome-associated conditions
    D. personality disorders

24. Which of the following is LEAST likely to be an area of deficit for a person with cerebral palsy?

    A. Independent living
    B. Learning
    C. Self-direction
    D. Self-care

25. The focus of most community-living skills instruction programs for developmentally disabled clients has tended to be
    A. telephone usage and money management
    B. language and socialization
    C. toileting and etiquette
    D. fire safety and mobility

KEY (CORRECT ANSWERS)

1.	C		11.	B
2.	B		12.	B
3.	C		13.	D
4.	D		14.	C
5.	B		15.	B
6.	A		16.	B
7.	B		17.	A
8.	B		18.	B
9.	A		19.	C
10.	C		20.	A

21. C
22. B
23. B
24. C
25. A

EXAMINATION SECTION
TEST 1

DIRECTIONS: Each question or incomplete statement is followed by several suggested answers or completions. Select the one that BEST answers the question or completes the statement. *PRINT THE LETTER OF THE CORRECT ANSWER IN THE SPACE AT THE RIGHT.*

1. It is generally accepted that, of the following, the MOST important medium for developing integration and continuity in learning on the job is
   A. day-to-day experience on the job
   B. the supervisory conference
   C. the staff meeting
   D. the professional seminar

   1.____

2. Assume that you find that one of your workers is over-identifying with a particular client.
   Of the following, the MOST appropriate step for you to take FIRST in dealing with this situation is to
   A. transfer the cases to another worker
   B. inform the worker that he cannot give satisfactory service if he over-identifies with a client
   C. interview the client yourself to determine his feelings about his relationship with the worker
   D. arrange a conference with the worker to discuss the reasons for her over-identification with this client

   2.____

3. The one of the following which is the MOST likely reason why a newly-appointed supervisor would have a tendency to interfere actively in a relationship between one of his workers and a client is that the supervisor
   A. has unresolved feelings about relinquishing the role of worker, and has not yet accepted his role as supervisor
   B. must give direct assistance in the situation because the worker cannot handle it
   C. is attempting to share with his worker the knowledge and skill which he has developed in direct practice
   D. has not realized that immediate responsibility for work with clients has been delegated to others

   3.____

4. A worker who has a tendency to resist authority and supervision can be helped MOST effectively if, of the following, the supervisor
   A. behaves in a strict and impersonal manner so that the worker will accept his authority as a supervisor
   B. modifies the relationship so that he will be less authoritarian and threatening to the worker
   C. gives the worker a simple, matter-of-fact interpretation of the supervisory relationship and has an understanding acceptance of the worker's response
   D. temporarily establishes a peer relationship with the worker in order to overcome his resistance

   4.____

5. Before interviewing a newly-appointed worker for the first time, of the following, it is DESIRABLE for the supervisor to
   A. learn as much as he can about the worker's background and interests in order to eliminate the routine of asking questions and eliciting answers
   B. review the job information to be covered in order to make it easier to be impersonal and keep to the business at hand
   C. send the worker orientation material about the agency and the job and ask him to study it before the interview
   D. review available information about the worker in order to find an area of shared experience to serve as a *taking off* point for getting acquainted

6. In interviewing a new worker, of the following, it is IMPORTANT for the supervisor to
   A. give direction to the progress of the interview and maintain a leadership role throughout
   B. allow the worker to take the initiative in order to give him full scope for freedom of expression
   C. maintain a non-directional approach so that the worker will reveal his true attitudes and feelings
   D. avoid interrupting the worker, even though he seems to want to do all the talking

7. When a new worker, during his first few days, shows such symptoms of insecurity as *stage fright*, helpless immobility, or extreme talkativeness, of the following, it would be MOST helpful for the supervisor to
   A. start the worker out on some activity in which he is relatively secure
   B. ignore the symptoms and allow the worker to *sink or swim* on his own
   C. have a conference with the worker and interpret to him the reasons for his feelings of insecurity
   D. consider the probability that this worker may not be suited for a profession which requires skill in interpersonal relationships

8. Of the following, the MOST desirable method of minimizing workers' dependence on the supervisor and encouraging self-dependence is to
   A. hold group instead of individual supervisory conferences at regular intervals
   B. schedule individual supervisory conferences only in response to the workers' obvious need for guidance
   C. plan for progressive exposure to other opportunities for learning afforded by the agency and the community
   D. allow workers to learn by trial and error rather than by direct supervisory guidance

9. Of the following, it would NOT be appropriate for the supervisor to use early supervisory conferences with the new workers as a means of
   A. giving him direct practical help in order to get going on the job
   B. estimating the level of his native abilities, professional skills and experience
   C. getting clues as to his characteristic ways of learning in a new situation
   D. assessing his potential for future supervisory responsibility

10. Without careful planning by the supervisor for orientation of the new worker, an informal system of orientation by co-workers inevitably develops.
Such an informal system of orientation is USUALLY
    A. *beneficial*, because many new workers learn more readily when instructed by their peers
    B. *harmful*, because informal orientation by an undesignated co-worker can lead a new worker astray instead of helping him
    C. *beneficial*, because assumption by subordinates of responsibility for orientation will free the supervisor for other urgent work
    D. *harmful*, because such informal orientation by a co-worker will tend to destroy the authority of the supervisor

10.____

11. Of the following, the BEST way for a supervisor to assist a subordinate who has unusual work pressures is to
    A. relieve him of some of his cases until the pressures subside
    B. help him to decide which cases should be given the most attention during the period of pressure, and how to provide coverage for less urgent cases
    C. inform him that he must learn to tolerate and adjust to such pressures
    D. point out that he should learn to understand the causes of the pressures, which probably resulted from his own deficiencies

11.____

12. Many supervisors have a tendency to use case records mainly for the purpose of analysis of the workers' skill or evaluation of their performance.
Of the following, a PROBABLE result of this practice is that
    A. workers are likely to tie-in recording with supervisory evaluation of their work, without giving proper emphasis to their importance in improving service to clients
    B. the worker is likely to devote an inordinate amount of time to case records at the expense of his clients
    C. the records are likely to be too lengthy and detailed, limiting their value for other important purposes
    D. the records are likely to be of little value for administrative and research purposes

12.____

13. A common obstacle to adequate recording in a large social work agency is the fact that many workers consider recording to be a time-consuming chore.
In order to obtain the cooperation of staff in keeping proper records, of the following, it is MOST important for an agency to provide
    A. indisputable evidence of the intelligent use of records as tools in formulating policy and improving service
    B. a system of checks and controls to assure that workers are preparing adequate and timely records
    C. adequate clerical services and mechanical equipment for recording
    D. sufficient time for recording in the organization of every job

13.____

14. The one of the following which is NOT a purpose of keeping case records in an agency is
    A. planning   B. research
    C. training   D. job classification

14.____

4 (#1)

15. When a supervisor is reviewing the records of a worker, of the following, he should plan to read
    A. records of new cases only, following up each interview selectively
    B. the total caseload, in order to determine which aspects of the worker's performance should be examined
    C. those records which the worker has brought to the supervisor's attention because of the need for help
    D. a block of records selected according to the worker's need for help, and some records selected at random

16. The one of the following which is the PRIMARY purpose of the regular staff meeting in an agency is
    A. initiation of action in order to get the agency's work done
    B. staff training and development
    C. program and policy determination
    D. communication of new policies and procedures

17. Of the following, group supervision in an agency is intended as a means of
    A. strengthening the total supervisory process
    B. shifting the focus of supervision from the individual to the group
    C. saving costs in terms of time and manpower
    D. influencing policy through group interaction

18. The supervisor's job brings him closer to such limiting factors in the operation of an agency as faulty administrative structure, shortage of funds and lack of facilities, inadequacies in personnel practices, community pressures, and excessive workload.
    For the supervisor to make a practice of communicating to his subordinates his feelings of frustration about such limitations in the work setting would be
    A. *appropriate*, because the worker will be more understanding of the supervisor's burdens and frustrations
    B. *inappropriate*, because the climate created will block rather than further the purposes of supervision
    C. *appropriate*, because such communication will create a more democratic climate between the worker and the supervisor
    D. *inappropriate*, because the supervisor must support and condone agency policies and practices in the presence of subordinates

19. A suggestion has been made that the teaching and administrative functions of supervision should be separated, so that the supervisor responsible for teaching would not be responsible for evaluation of the same workers.
    The one of the following which is the MOST important reason for this point of view is that
    A. elements that confer on the supervisor a position of authority and power unduly threaten the learning situation
    B. teaching skill and administrative ability do not usually go together

C. a supervisor who has been responsible for training a worker is likely to be prejudiced in his favor
D. performance evaluation and total job accountability should be two separate functions

20. In reviewing a worker's cases in preparation for a periodic evaluation, you note that she has done a uniformly good job with certain types of cases and poor work with other types of cases.
Of the following, the BEST approach for you to take in this situation is to
   A. bring this to the worker's attention, find out why she favors certain types of clients, and discuss ways in which she can improve her service to all clients
   B. bring this to the worker's attention and suggest that she may need professional counseling, as she seems to be blocked in working with certain types of cases
   C. assign to her mainly those cases which she handles best and transfer the types of cases which she handles poorly to another worker
   D. accept the fact that a worker cannot be expected to give uniformly good service to all clients, and take no further action

20.____

KEY (CORRECT ANSWERS)

1.	B	11.	B
2.	D	12.	A
3.	A	13.	A
4.	C	14.	D
5.	D	15.	D
6.	A	16.	A
7.	A	17.	A
8.	C	18.	B
9.	D	19.	A
10.	B	20.	A

TEST 2

DIRECTIONS: Each question or incomplete statement is followed by several suggested answers or completions. Select the one that BEST answers the question or completes the statement. *PRINT THE LETTER OF THE CORRECT ANSWER IN THE SPACE AT THE RIGHT.*

1. Of the following, the choice of method to be used in the supervisory process should be influenced MOST by the
   A. number and type of cases carried by each worker
   B. emotional maturity of the worker
   C. number of workers supervised and their past experience
   D. subject matter to be learned and the long-range goals of supervision

   1.____

2. In an evaluation conference with a worker, the BEST approach for the supervisor to take is to
   A. help the worker to identify his strengths as a basis for working on his weaknesses
   B. identify the worker's weaknesses and help him overcome them
   C. allow the worker to identify his weaknesses first and then suggest ways of overcoming them
   D. discuss the worker's weaknesses but emphasize his strengths

   2.____

3. Assume that a worker is discouraged about the progress of his work and feels that it is futile to attempt to cope with many of his cases.
   Of the following, it would be BEST for the supervisor to
   A. suggest to the worker that such feelings are inappropriate for a professional worker
   B. tell the worker that he must seek professional help in order to overcome these feelings
   C. reduce the worker's caseload and give him cases that are less complex
   D. review with the worker several of his cases in which there were obvious accomplishments

   3.____

4. The supervisor is responsible for providing the worker with the following means of support, with the EXCEPTION of
   A. interest and advice on his personal problems
   B. instruction on community resources
   C. inspiration for carrying out the work of the agency
   D. understanding his strengths and limitations

   4.____

5. When a worker frequently takes the initiative in asking questions and discussing problems during a supervisory conference, this is PROBABLY an indication that the
   A. supervisor is not sufficiently interested in the work
   B. conference is a positive learning experience for the worker
   C. worker is hostile and resists supervision
   D. supervisor's position of authority is in question

   5.____

6. When a supervisor finds that one of his workers cannot accept criticism, of the following, it would be BEST for the supervisor to
   A. have the worker transferred to another supervisor
   B. warn the worker of disciplinary proceedings unless his attitude changes
   C. have the worker suspended after explaining the reason
   D. explore with the worker his attitude toward authority

7. Of the following, the condition which the inexperienced worker is LEAST likely to be aware of, without the guidance of the supervisor, is
   A. when he is successful in helping a client
   B. when he is not making progress in helping a client
   C. that he has a personal bias toward certain clients
   D. that he feels insecure because of lack of experience

8. The supervisor should provide an inexperienced worker with controls as well as freedom MAINLY because controls will
   A. enable him to set up his own controls sooner
   B. put him in a situation which is closer to the realities of life
   C. help him to use authority in handling a casework problem
   D. give him a feeling of security and lay the foundation for future self-direction

9. A result of the use of summarized case recording by the worker is that it
   A. gives the supervisor more responsibility for selecting cases to discuss in conference
   B. makes more time available for other activities
   C. lowers the morale of many workers
   D. decreases discussion of cases by the worker and the supervisor

10. The distinction between the role of professional workers and the role of auxiliary or sub-professional workers in an agency is based upon the
    A. position within the agency hierarchy
    B. amount of close supervision given
    C. emergent nature of tasks assigned
    D. functions performed

11. Of the following, the MOST important source of learning for the worker should be
    A. departmental directives and professional literature
    B. his co-workers in the agency
    C. the content of in-service training courses
    D. the clients in his caseload

12. A client is MOST likely to feel that he is receiving acceptance and understanding if the social worker
    A. gets detailed information about the client's problem
    B. demonstrates that he realistically understands the client's problem
    C. has an intellectual understanding of the client's problem
    D. offers the client assurance of assistance

13. A client will be MORE encouraged to speak freely about his problems if the worker
    A. avoids asking too many questions
    B. asks leading rather than pointed questions
    C. suggests possible answers
    D. identifies with the client

14. A client would be MOST likely to be able to accept help in a time of crisis and need if the worker
    A. explains agency policy to him
    B. responds immediately to the client's need
    C. explains why help cannot be given immediately
    D. reaches out to help the client establish his rightful claim for assistance

15. It is a generally accepted principle that the worker should interpret for himself what the client is saying, but usually should not pass his interpretation on to the client because the client
    A. will become hostile to the worker
    B. should arrive at his own conclusions at his own pace
    C. must request the interpretation first
    D. usually wants facts, rather than the worker's interpretation

16. In evaluating the client's capacity to cope with his problems, it is MOST important for the worker to assess his ability to
    A. form close relationships   B. ask for help
    C. express his hostility   D. verbalize his difficulties

17. When a worker finds that he disagrees strongly with an agency policy, it is DESIRABLE for him to
    A. share his feelings about the policy with his client
    B. understand fully why he has such strong feelings about the policy
    C. refer cases involving the policy to his supervisor
    D. refuse to give help in cases involving the policy

18. Which of the following practices is BEST for a supervisor to use when assigning work to his staff?
    A. Give workers with seniority the most difficult jobs
    B. Assign all unimportant work to the slower workers
    C. Permit each employee to pick the job he prefers
    D. Make assignments based on the workers' abilities

19. In which of the following instances is a supervisor MOST justified in giving commands to people under his supervision?
    When
    A. they delay in following instructions which have been given to them clearly
    B. they become relaxed and slow about work, and he wants to speed up their production
    C. he must direct them in an emergency situation
    D. he is instructing them on jobs that are unfamiliar to them

20. Which of the following supervisory actions or attitudes is MOST likely to result in getting subordinates to try to do as much work as possible for a supervisor?
    He
    A. shows that his most important interest is in schedules and production goals
    B. consistently pressures his staff to get the work out
    C. never fails to let them know he is in charge
    D. considers their abilities and needs while requiring that production goals be met

20.____

KEY (CORRECT ANSWERS)

1.	D	11.	D
2.	A	12.	B
3.	D	13.	D
4.	A	14.	D
5.	B	15.	B
6.	D	16.	A
7.	C	17.	B
8.	D	18.	D
9.	B	19.	C
10.	D	20.	D

TEST 3

DIRECTIONS: Each question or incomplete statement is followed by several suggested answers or completions. Select the one that BEST answers the question or completes the statement. *PRINT THE LETTER OF THE CORRECT ANSWER IN THE SPACE AT THE RIGHT.*

1. One of your workers comes to you and complains in an angry manner about your having chosen him for some particular assignment. In your opinion, the subject of the complaint is trivial land unimportant, but it seems to be quite important to your worker.
   The BEST of the following actions for you to take in this situation is to
   A. allow the worker to continue talking until he has calmed down and then explain the reasons for your having chosen him for that particular assignment
   B. warn the worker to moderate his tone of voice at once because he is bordering on insubordination
   C. tell the worker in a friendly tone that he is making a tremendous fuss over an extremely minor matter
   D. point out to the worker that you are his immediate supervisor and that you are running the unit in accordance with official policy

   1.____

2. The one of the following which is the LEAST desirable action for an assistant supervisor to take in disciplining a subordinate for an infraction of the rules is to
   A. caution him against repetition of the infraction, even if it is minor
   B. point out his progress in applying the rules at the same time that you reprimand him
   C. be as specific as possible in reprimanding him for rule infractions
   D. allow a cooling-off period to elapse before reprimanding him

   2.____

3. A training program for workers assigned to the intake section should include actual practice in simulated interviews under simulated conditions.
   The one of the following educational principles which is the CHIEF justification for this statement is that
   A. the workers will remember what they see better and longer than what they read or hear
   B. the workers will learn more effectively by actually doing the act themselves than they would learn from watching others do it
   C. the conduct of simulated interviews once or twice will enable them to cope with the real situation with little difficulty
   D. a training program must employ methods of a practical nature if the workers are to find anything of lasting value in it

   3.____

4. In order for a supervisor to employ the system of democratic leadership in his supervision, it would generally be BEST for him to
   A. allow his subordinates to assist in deciding on methods of work performance and job assignments but only in those areas where decisions have not been made on higher administrative levels

   4.____

B. allow his subordinates to decide how to do the required work, interposing his authority when work is not completed on schedule or is improperly completed
C. attempt to make assignments of work to individuals only of the type which they enjoy doing
D. maintain control over job assignment and work production, but allow the subordinates to select methods of work and internal conditions of work at democratically conducted staff conferences

5. In a unit in which supervision has been considered quite effective, it has become necessary to press for above-normal production for a limited period to achieve a required goal.
The one of the following which is a LEAST likely result of this pressure is that
    A. there will be more *griping* by employees
    B. some workers will do both more and better work than has been normal for them
    C. there will be an enhanced feeling of group unity
    D. there will be increased absenteeism

6. For a supervisor to encourage competitive feelings among his staff is
    A. *advisable*, chiefly because the workers will perform more efficiently when they have proper motivation
    B. *inadvisable*, chiefly because the workers will not perform well under the pressure of competition
    C. *advisable*, chiefly because the workers will have a greater incentive to perform their job properly
    D. *inadvisable*, chiefly because the workers may focus their attention on areas where they excel and neglect other essential aspects of the job

7. In selecting jobs to be assigned to a new worker, the supervisor should assign those jobs which
    A. give the worker the greatest variety of experience
    B. offer the worker the greatest opportunity to achieve concrete results
    C. present the worker with the greatest stimulation because of their interesting nature
    D. require the least amount of contact with outside agencies

8. A supervisor should avoid a detailed discussion of a worker-client interview with a new worker before the worker has fully recorded the interview CHIEFLY because such a discussion might
    A. cover matters which are already fully covered and explained in the written record
    B. make the worker forget some important deal learned during the interview
    C. color the recording according to the worker's reaction to his supervisor's opinions
    D. minimize the worker's feeling of having reached a decision independently

9. Some supervisors encourage their worker to submit a list of their questions about specific jobs or their comments about problems they wish to discuss in advance of the worker-supervisor conference.
   This practice is
   A. *desirable*, chiefly because it helps to stimulate and focus the worker's thinking about his caseload
   B. *undesirable*, chiefly because it will stifle the worker's free expression of his problems and attitudes
   C. *desirable,* chiefly because it will allow the conference to move along more smoothly and quickly
   D. *undesirable*, chiefly because it will restrict the scope of the conference and the variety of jobs discussed

10. An alert supervisor hears a worker apparently giving the wrong information to a client and immediately reprimands him severely.
    For the supervisor to reprimand the worker at his point is poor CHIEFLY because
    A. instruction must precede correct performance
    B. oral reprimands are less effective than written reprimands
    C. the worker was given no opportunity to explain his reasons for what he did
    D. more effective training can be obtained by discussing the errors with a group of workers

11. The one of the following circumstances when it would generally be MOST proper for a supervisor to do a job himself rather than to train a subordinate to do the job is when it is
    A. a job which the supervisor enjoys doing and does well
    B. not a very time-consuming job but an important one
    C. difficult to train another to do the job, yet is not difficult for the supervisor to do
    D. unlikely that this or any similar job will have to be done again at any future time

12. Effective training of subordinates requires that the supervisor understand certain facts about learning and forgetting processes.
    Among these is the fact that people GENERALLY
    A. forget what they learned at a much greater rate during the first day than during subsequent periods
    B. both learn and forget at a relatively constant rate and this rate is dependent upon their general intellectual capacity
    C. learn at a relatively constant rate except for periods of assimilation when the quantity of retained learning decreases while information is becoming firmly fixed in the mind
    D. learn very slowly at first when introduced to a new topic, after which there is a great increase in the rate of learning

13. It has been suggested that a subordinate who likes his superior will tend to do better work than one who does not.
    According to the MOST widely held current theories of supervision, this suggestion is a
    A. *bad* one, since personal relationships tend to interfere with proper professional relationships
    B. *bad* one, since the strongest motivating factors are fear and uncertainty
    C. *good* one, since liking one's superior is a motivating factor for good work performance
    D. *good* one, since liking one's supervisor is the most important factor in employee performance

14. One factor which might be given consideration in deciding upon the optimum span of control of a supervisor over his immediate subordinates is the position of the supervisor in the hierarchy of the organization.
    It is generally considered proper that the number of subordinates immediately supervised by a higher, upper echelon supervisor _____ the number supervised by lower level supervisors.
    A. is unrelated to and tends to form no pattern with
    B. should be about the same as
    C. should be larger than
    D. should be smaller than

15. The one of the following instances when it is MOST important for an upper level supervisor to follow the chain of command is when he is
    A. communicating decisions   B. communicating information
    C. receiving suggestions   D. seeking information

16. At the end of his probationary period, a supervisor should be considered potentially valuable in his position if he shows
    A. awareness of his areas of strength and weakness, identification with the administration of the department, and ability to learn under supervision
    B. skill in work, supervision, and administration, and a friendly democratic approach to the staff
    C. knowledge of departmental policies and procedures and ability to carry them out, ability to use authority, and ability to direct the work of the staff
    D. an identification with the department, acceptance of responsibility, and ability to give help to the individuals who are to be supervised

17. Good supervision is selective because
    A. it is not necessary to direct all the activities of the person
    B. a supervisor would never have time to know the whole caseload of a worker
    C. workers resent too much help from a supervisor
    D. too much reading is a waste of valuable time

18. An important administrative problem is how precisely to define the limits of authority that is delegated to subordinate supervisors.
    Such definition of limits of authority should be
    A. as precise as possible and practicable in all areas
    B. as precise as possible and practicable in areas of function, but should allow considerable flexibility in the area of personnel management
    C. as precise as possible and practicable in the area
    D. of personnel management, but should allow considerable flexibility in the areas of function
    E. in general terms so as to allow considerable flexibility both in the areas of function and in the areas of personnel management

19. Experts in the field of personnel relations feel that it is generally a bad practice for subordinate employees to become aware of pending or contemplated changes in policy or organizational set-up via the *grapevine* CHIEFLY because
    A. evidence that one or more responsible officials have proved untrustworthy will undermine confidence in the agency
    B. the information disseminated by this method is seldom entirely accurate and generally spreads needless unrest among the subordinate staff
    C. the subordinate staff may conclude that the administration feels the staff cannot be trusted with the true information
    D. the subordinate staff may conclude that the administration lacks the courage to make an unpopular announcement through official channels

20. Supervision is subject to many interpretations, depending on the area in which it functions.
    Of the following, the statement which represents the MOST appropriate meaning of supervision as it is known in social work practice is that it
    A. is a leadership process for the development of new leaders
    B. is an educational and administrative process aimed at teaching personnel the goal of improved service to the client
    C. is an activity aimed chiefly at insuring that workers will adhere to all agency directives
    D. provides the opportunity for administration to secure staff reaction to agency policies

21. A supervisor may utilize various methods in the supervisory process.
    The one of the following upon which sound supervisory practice rests in the selection of supervisory techniques is
    A. an estimate of the worker arrived at through current and past evaluation of performance as well as through worker's participation
    B. the previous supervisor's evaluation and recommendation
    C. the worker's expression of his personal preference for certain types of experience
    D. the amount of time available to supervisor and supervisee

22. It is the practice of some supervisors, when they believe that it would be desirable for a subordinate to take a particular action in a case, to inform the subordinate of this in the form of a suggestion rather than in the form of a direct order.
    In general, this method of getting a subordinate to take the desired action is
    A. *inadvisable*; it may create in the mind of the subordinate the impression that the supervisor is uncertain about the efficacy of her plan and is trying to avoid whatever responsibility she may have in resolving the case
    B. *advisable*; it provides the subordinate with the maximum opportunity to use her own judgment in handling the case
    C. *inadvisable*; it provides the subordinate with no clear-cut direction and, therefore, is likely to leave her with a feeling of uncertainty and frustration
    D. *advisable*; it presents the supervisor's view in a manner which will be most likely to evoke the subordinate's cooperation

23. A veteran supervisor noticed that one of her workers of average ability had begun developing some bad work habits, becoming especially careless in her recordkeeping. After reprimand from the supervisor, the investigator corrected her errors and has been doing satisfactory work since then.
    For the supervisor to keep referring to this period of poor work during her weekly conferences with this employee would generally be considered poor personnel practice CHIEFLY because
    A. praise rather than criticism is generally the best method to use in improving the work of an unsatisfactory worker
    B. the supervisor cannot know whether the employee's errors will follow an established pattern
    C. the fault which evoked the original negative criticism no longer exists
    D. this would tend to frustrate the worker by making her strive overly hard to reach a level of productivity which is beyond her ability to achieve

24. Assume that you are now a supervisor in a specific unit. Two experienced investigators in your unit, both of whom do above average work, have for some time not gotten along with each other for personal reasons Their attitude toward one another has suddenly become hostile and noisy disagreement has taken place in the office.
    The BEST action for you to take FIRST in this situation is to
    A. transfer one of the two investigators to another unit where contact with the other investigator will be unnecessary
    B. discuss the problem with the two investigators together, insisting that they confide in you and tell you the cause of their mutual antagonism
    C. confer with the two investigators separately, pointing out to each the need to adopt an adult professional attitude with respect to their on-the-job relations
    D. advise the two investigators that should the situation grow worse, disciplinary action will be considered

25. It has long been recognized that relationships exist between worker morale and working conditions.
The one of the following which BEST clarifies these existing relationships is that morale is
   A. affected for better or worse in direct relationship to the magnitude of the changes in working conditions for better or worse
   B. better when working conditions are better
   C. little affected by working conditions so long as the working conditions do not approach the intolerable
   D. more affected by the degree of interest shown in providing good working conditions than by the actual conditions and may, perversely, be highest when working conditions are worst

25._____

KEY (CORRECT ANSWERS)

1.	A		11.	D
2.	D		12.	A
3.	B		13.	C
4.	A		14.	D
5.	D		15.	A
6.	D		16.	D
7.	B		17.	A
8.	C		18.	A
9.	A		19.	B
10.	C		20.	B

21. A
22. D
23. C
24. C
25. D

SUPERVISION, ADMINISTRATION, MANAGEMENT, AND ORGANIZATION

EXAMINATION SECTION

TEST 1

DIRECTIONS: Each question or incomplete statement is followed by several suggested answers or completions. Select the one that BEST answers the question or completes the statement. *PRINT THE LETTER OF THE CORRECT ANSWER IN THE SPACE AT THE RIGHT.*

1. A supervisor scheduled and interview with a subordinate in order to discuss his unsatisfactory performance during the previous several weeks. The subordinate's work contained an excessive number of careless errors.
   After the interview, the supervisor, reviewing his own approach for self-examination, listed three techniques he had used in the interview, as follows:
   I. Specifically pointed out to the subordinate where he had failed to meet the standards expected.
   II. Shared the blame for certain management errors that had irritated the subordinate.
   III. Agreed with the subordinate on specific targets to be met during the period ahead.
   Of the following statements, the one that is MOST acceptable concerning the above three techniques is that
   A. all 3 techniques are correct
   B. techniques I and II are correct; III is not correct
   C. techniques II and III are correct; I is not correct
   D. techniques I and III are correct; II is not correct

2. Assume that the performance of an employee is not satisfactory.
   Of the following, the MOST effective way for a supervisor to attempt to improve the performance of the employee is to meet with him and to
   A. order him to change his behavior
   B. indicate the actions that are unsatisfactory and the penalties for them
   C. show him alternate ways of behaving and a method for him to evaluate his attempts at change
   D. suggest that he use the behavior of the supervisor as a model of acceptable conduct

3. Training employees to be productive workers is based on four fundamental principles:
   I. Demonstrate how the job should be done by telling and showing the correct operations step-by-step
   II. Allow the employee to get some of the feel of the job by allowing him to try it a bit
   III. Put him on the job while continuing to check his performance
   IV. Let him know why the job is important and why it must be done right

The MOST logical order for these training steps is:
A. I, III, II, IV   B. I, IV, II, III   C. II, I, III, IV   D. IV, I, II, III

4. Sometimes a supervisor is faced with the need to train under-educated new employees.
The following five statements relate to training such employees.
I. Make the training general rather than specific
II. Rely upon demonstrations and illustrations whenever possible
III. Overtrain rather than undertrain by erring on the side of imparting a little more skill than is absolutely necessary
IV. Provide lots of follow-up on the job
V. Reassure and recognize frequently in order to increase self-confidence
Which of the following choices lists all the above statements that are generally CORRECT?
A. I, II, IV   B. II, III, IV, V   C. I, II, V   D. I, II, IV, V

5. One of the ways in which some supervisors train subordinates is to discuss the subordinate's weaknesses with them. Experts who have explored the actual feelings and reactions of subordinates in such situations have come to the conclusion that such interviews USUALLY
A. are seen by subordinates as a threat to their self-esteem
B. give subordinates a feeling of importance which leads to better learning
C. convince subordinates to accept the opinion of the supervisor
D. result in the development of better supervision

6. The one of the following which BEST describes the rate at which a trainee learns departmental procedures is that he *probably* will learn
A. at the same rate throughout if the material to be learned is complex
B. slowly in the beginning and then learning will accelerate steadily
C. quickly for a while, than slow down temporarily
D. at the same rate if the material to be learned is lengthy

7. Which of the following statements concerning the delegation of work to subordinate employees is generally CORRECT?
A. A supervisor's personal attitude toward delegation has a minimal effect on his skill in delegating.
B. A willingness to let subordinates make mistakes has a place in work delegation.
C. The element of trust has little impact on the effectiveness of work delegation.
D. The establishment of controls does not enhance the process of delegation.

8. Assume that you are the chairman of a group that has been formed to discuss and solve a particular problem. After a half-hour of discussion, you feel that the group is wandering off the point and is no longer discussing the problem.
In this situation, it would be BEST for you to
A. wait to see whether the group will get back on the track by itself
B. ask the group to stop and to try a different approach

C. ask the group to stop, decide where they are going, and then to decide how to continue
D. ask the group to stop, decide where they are going, and then to continue in a different direction

9. One method of group decision-making is the use of committees. Following are four statements concerning committees.
   I. Considering the value of each individual member's time, committees are costly.
   II. One result of committee decisions is that no one may be held responsible for the decision.
   III. Committees will make decisions more promptly than individuals.
   IV. Committee decisions tend to be balanced and to take different viewpoints into account.
   Which of the following choices lists all of the above statements that are generally CORRECT?
   A. I and II   B. II and III   C. I, II, IV   D. II, III, IV

10. Assume that an employee bypasses his supervisor and comes directly to you, the superior officer, to ask for a short leave of absence because of a pressing personal problem. The employee did not first consult with his immediate supervisor because he believes that his supervisor is unfavorably biased against him.
    Of the following, the MOST desirable way for you to handle this situation is to
    A. instruct the employee that is it not appropriate for him to go over the head of his supervisor regardless of their personal relationship
    B. listen to a brief description of his problem and then tactfully suggest that he take the matter up with his supervisor before coming to you
    C. request that both the employee and his supervisor meet jointly with you in order to discuss the employee's problem and to get at the reasons behind their apparent difficulty
    D. listen carefully to the employee's problem and then, without committing yourself one way or the other, promise to discuss it with his supervisor

11. Which of the following statements concerning the motivation of subordinates is generally INCORRECT? The
    A. authoritarian approach as the method of supervision is likely to result in the setting of minimal performance standards for themselves by subordinates
    B. encouragement of competition among subordinates may lead to deterioration of teamwork
    C. granting of benefits by a supervisor to subordinates in order to gain their gratitude will result in maximum output by the subordinates
    D. opportunity to achieve job satisfaction has an important effect on motivating subordinates

4 (#1)

12. Of the following, the MOST serious disadvantage of having a supervisor evaluate subordinates on the basis of measurable performance goals that are set jointly by the supervisor and the subordinates is that this results-oriented appraisal method   12._____
    A. focuses on past performance rather than plans for the future
    B. fails to provide sufficient feedback to help subordinates learn where they stand
    C. encourages the subordinates to conceal poor performance and set low goals
    D. changes the primary task of the supervisor from helping subordinates improve to criticizing their performance

13. A supervisor can BEST provide on-the-job satisfaction for his subordinates by   13._____
    A. providing rewards for good performance
    B. allowing them to decide when to do the assigned work
    C. motivating them to perform according to accepted procedures
    D. providing challenging work that achieves departmental objectives

14. Which of the following factors generally contributes MOST to job satisfaction among supervisory employees?   14._____
    A. Autonomy and independence on the job
    B. Job security
    C. Pleasant physical working conditions
    D. Adequate economic rewards

15. Large bureaucracies typically exhibit certain characteristics.
    Of the following, it would be CORRECT to state that such bureaucracies generally   15._____
    A. tend to oversimplify communications
    B. pay undue attention to informal organizations
    C. develop an attitude of "group-think" and conformity
    D. emphasize personal growth among employees

16. When positive methods fail to achieve conformity with accepted standards of conduct or performance, a negative type of action, punitive in nature, usually must follow.
    The one of the following that is usually considered LEAST important for the success of such punishment or negative discipline is that it be   16._____
    A. certain   B. swift   C. severe   D. consistent

17. Assume that you are a supervisor. Philip Smith, who is under your supervision, informs you that James Jones, who is also your subordinate, has been creating antagonism and friction within the unit because of his unnecessarily gruff manner in dealing with his co-workers. Smith's remarks confirm your own observations of Jones' behavior and its effects.   17._____

56

In handling this situation, the one of the following procedures which will probably be MOST effective is to
A. ask Smith to act as an informal counselor to Jones and report the results to you
B. counsel the other employees in your unit on methods of changing attitudes of people
C. interview Jones and help him to understand this problem
D. order Jones to carry out his responsibilities with greater consideration for the feelings of his co-workers

18. The principle relating to the number of subordinates who can be supervised effectively by one supervisor is COMMONLY known as
    A. span of control   B. delegation of authority
    C. optimum personnel assignment   D. organizational factor

18.____

19. Ascertaining and improving the level of morale in a public agency is one of the responsibilities of a conscientious supervisor.
The one of the following aspects of subordinates' behavior which is NOT an indication of low morale is
    A. lower-level employees participating in organizational decision-making
    B. careless treatment of equipment
    C. general deterioration of personal appearance
    D. formation of cliques

19.____

20. Employees may resist changes in agency operations even though such changes are often necessary. If you, as a supervisor, are attempting to introduce a necessary change, you should first fully explain the reasons for it to your staff.
Your NEXT step should be to
    A. set specific goals and outline programs for all employees
    B. invite employee participation in effectuating the change by asking for suggestions to accomplish it
    C. discuss the need for improved work performance by city employees
    D. point out the penalties for non-cooperation without singling out any employee by name

20.____

21. A supervisor should normally void giving orders in an offhand or casual manner MAINLY because his subordinates
    A. are like most people and may resent being treated lightly
    B. may attach little importance to these orders
    C. may work best if given the choice of work methods
    D. are unlikely to need instructions in most matters

21.____

22. Assume that, as a supervisor, you have just praised a subordinate. While he expresses satisfaction at your praise, he complains that it does not help him get promoted even though he is on a promotion eligible list, since there is no current vacancy.

22.____

In these circumstances, it would be BEST for you to
- A. minimize the importance of advancement and emphasize the satisfaction in the work itself
- B. follow up by pointing out some errors he has committed in the past
- C. admit that the situation exists, and express the hope that it will improve
- D. tell him that, until quite recently, advancement was even slower

23. Departmental policies are usually broad rules or guides for action. It is important for a supervisor to understand his role with respect to policy implementation.
Of the following, the MOST accurate description of this role is that a supervisor should
- A. be apologetic toward his subordinates when applying unpopular policies to them
- B. act within policy limits, although he can attempt to influence policy change by making his thoughts and observations known to his superior
- C. arrange his activities so that he is able to deal simultaneously with situations that involve several policy matters
- D. refrain as much as possible from exercising permissible discretion in applying policy to matters under his control

23.____

24. A supervisor should be aware that most subordinates will ask questions at meetings or group discussions in order to
- A. stimulate other employees to express their opinions
- B. discover how they may be affected by the subjects under discussion
- C. display their knowledge of the topics under discussion
- D. consume time in order to avoid returning to their normal tasks

24.____

25. Don't assign responsibilities with conflicting objectives to the same work group. For example, to require a unit to monitor the quality of its own work is a bad practice.
This practice is MOST likely to be bad because
- A. the chain of command will be unnecessarily lengthened
- B. it is difficult to portray mixed duties accurately on an organization chart
- C. employees may act in collusion to cover up poor work
- D. the supervisor may delegate responsibilities which he should retain

25.____

KEY (CORRECT ANSWERS)

1.	A	11.	C
2.	C	12.	C
3.	D	13.	D
4.	B	14.	A
5.	A	15.	C
6.	C	16.	C
7.	B	17.	C
8.	C	18.	A
9.	C	19.	A
10.	D	20.	B

21. B
22. C
23. B
24. B
25. C

TEST 2

DIRECTIONS: Each question or incomplete statement is followed by several suggested answers or completions. Select the one that BEST answers the question or completes the statement. *PRINT THE LETTER OF THE CORRECT ANSWER IN THE SPACE AT THE RIGHT.*

1. Some supervisors use an approach in which each phase of the job is explained in broad terms supervision is general, and employees are allowed broad discretion in performing their job duties.
   Such a supervisory approach USUALLY affects employee motivation by
   A. improving morale and providing an incentive to work harder
   B. providing little or no incentive to work harder than the minimum required
   C. creating extra pressure, usually resulting in decreased performance
   D. reducing incentive to work and causing employees to feel neglected, particularly in performing complex tasks

   1.____

2. An employee complains to a superior officer that he has been treated unfairly by his supervisor, stating that other employees have been given less work to do and shown other forms of favoritism.
   Of the following, the BEST thing for the superior officer to do FIRST in order to handle this problem is to
   A. try to discover whether the subordinate has a valid complaint or if something else is the real problem
   B. ask other employees whether they feel their treatment is consistent and fair
   C. ask his supervisor to explain the charges
   D. see that the number of cases assigned to this employee is reduced

   2.____

3. Of the following, the MOST important condition needed to help a group of people to work well together and get the job done is
   A. higher salaries and a better working environment
   B. enough free time to relieve the tension
   C. good communication among everyone involved in the job
   D. assurance that everyone likes the work

   3.____

4. A supervisor realizes that a subordinate has called in sick for three Mondays out of the past four. These absences have interfered with staff performance and have been part of the cause of the unit's "behind schedule" condition.
   In order to correct this situation, it would be BEST for the supervisor to
   A. order the subordinate to explain his abuse of sick leave
   B. discuss with the subordinate the penalties for abusing sick leave
   C. discuss the matter with his own supervisor
   D. ask the subordinate in private whether he has a problem about coming to work

   4.____

5. Of the following, the MOST effective way for a supervisor to minimize undesirable rumors about new policies in the units under his supervision is to
   A. bypass the supervisor and communicate directly with the individual members of the units
   B. supply immediate and accurate information to everyone who is supposed to be informed
   C. play down the importance of the rumors
   D. issue all communications in written form

6. Which of the following is an indication that a superior officer is delegating authority PROPERLY?
   A. The superior officer closely checks the work of experienced subordinates at all stages in order to maintain standards.
   B. The superior officer gives overlapping assignments to insure that work is completed on time.
   C. The work of his subordinates can proceed and be completed during the superior officer's absence.
   D. The work of each supervisor is reviewed by him more than once in order to insure quality.

7. Of the following supervisory practices, the one which is MOST likely to foster employee morale is for the supervisor to
   A. take an active interest in subordinates' personal lives
   B. ignore mistakes
   C. give praise when justified
   D. permit rules to go unenforced occasionally

8. As the supervisor who is responsible for the implementation of new paperwork procedure, you note that the workers often do not follow the stipulated procedure.
   Before taking action, it would be ADVISABLE to realize that
   A. unconscious behavior, such as failure to adapt to change, is largely uncontrollable
   B. new procedures sometimes have to be modified and adapted after being tried out
   C. threats of disciplinary action will encourage approval of change
   D. procedures that fail should be abandoned and replaced

9. The one of the following which is generally considered to be the MOST significant criticism of the modern practice of effective human relations in management of large organizations is that human relations
   A. weakens management authority over employees
   B. gives employees control of operations
   C. can be used to manipulate and control employees
   D. weakens unions

10. Of the following, the MOST important reason why the supervisor should promote good supervisor-subordinate relations is to encourage his staff to
    A. feel important
    B. be more receptive to control
    C. be happy in their work
    D. meet production performance levels

11. A superior officer decides to assign a special report directly to an employee, bypassing his supervisor.
    In general, this practice is
    A. *advisable*, chiefly because it broadens the superior officer's span of authority
    B. *inadvisable*, chiefly because it undermines the authority of the supervisor in the eyes of his subordinates
    C. *advisable*, chiefly because it reduces the number of details the supervisor must know
    D. *inadvisable*, chiefly because it gives too much work to the employee

12. Many supervisors make it a practice to solicit suggestions from their subordinates and to encourage their participation in decision-making.
    The success of this type of supervision usually depends MOST directly upon the
    A. quality of leadership provided by the supervisor
    B. number of the supervisor's immediate subordinates
    C. availability of opportunities for employee advancement
    D. degree to which work assignments cause problems

13. Small informal groups or "cliques" often appear in a work setting.
    The one of the following which is generally an advantage of such groups, from an administrative point of view, is that they
    A. are not influenced by the administrative set-up of the office
    B. encourage socializing after working hours
    C. develop leadership roles among the office staff
    D. provide a "steam valve" for release of tension and fatigue

14. Assume that you are a superior officer in charge of several supervisors who, in turn, are in charge of a number of employees. The employees who are supervised by Jones (a supervisor) come as a group to you and indicate several reasons why Jones is incompetent and "has to go."
    Of the following, your BEST course of action to take FIRST is to
    A. direct the employees to see Jones about the matter
    B. suggest to the employees that they should attempt to work with Jones until he can be transferred
    C. discuss the possibility of terminating Jones with your superior
    D. ask Jones about the comments of the employees after they depart

15. Of the following, the MAIN effect which the delegation of authority can have on the efficiency of an organization is to
    A. reduce the risk of decision-making errors
    B. produce uniformity of policy and action
    C. facilitate speedier decisions and actions
    D. enable closer control of operations

16. Of the following, the main DISADVANTAGE of temporarily transferring a newly appointed worker to another unit because of an unexpected vacancy is that the temporary nature of his assignment will, MOST likely,
    A. undermine his incentive to orient himself to his new job
    B. interfere with his opportunities for future advancement
    C. result in friction between himself and his new co-workers
    D. place his new supervisor in a difficult and awkward position

17. Assume that you, as a supervisor, have decided to raise the quality of work produced by your subordinates.
    The BEST of the following procedures for you to follow is to
    A. develop mathematically precise standards
    B. appoint a committee of subordinates to set firm and exacting guidelines, including penalties for deviations
    C. modify standards developed by supervisors in other organizations
    D. provide consistent evaluation of subordinates' work, furnishing training whenever advisable

18. Assume that a supervisor under your supervision strongly objects whenever changes are proposed which would improve the efficiency of his unit.
    Of the following, the MOST desirable way for you to change his attitude is to
    A. involve him in the planning and formulation of changes
    B. promise to recommend him for a more challenging assignment if he accepts changes
    C. threaten to have him transferred to another unit if he does not accept changes
    D. ask him to go along with the changes on a tentative, trial basis

19. Work goals may be defined in terms of units produced or in terms of standards of performance.
    Which of the following statements concerning work goals is CORRECT?
    A. Workers who have a share in establishing goals tend to set a fairly high standard for themselves, but fail to work toward it.
    B. Workers tend to produce according to what they believe are the goals actually expected of them.
    C. Since workers usually produce less than the established goals, management should set goals higher than necessary.
    D. The individual differences of workers can be minimized by using strict goals and invariable procedures.

20. Of the following, the type of employee who would respond BEST to verbal instructions given in the form of a suggestion or wish is the
    A. experienced worker who is eager to please
    B. sensitive and emotional worker
    C. hostile worker who is somewhat lazy
    D. slow and methodical worker

21. As a supervisor, you note that the output of an experienced staff member has dropped dramatically during the last two months. In addition, his error rate is significantly above that of other staff members. When you ask the employee the reason for his poor performance, he says, "Well, it's rather personal and I would rather not talk about it if you don't mind."
    At this point, which of the following would be the BEST reply?
    A. Tell him that you will give him two weeks to improve or you will discuss the matter with your own supervisor
    B. Insist that he tell you the reason for his poor work and assure him that anything personal will be kept confidential
    C. Say that you don't want to interfere, but, at the same time, his work has deteriorated, and that you're concerned about it
    D. Explain in a friendly manner that you are going to place a warning letter in his personnel folder that states he has one month in which to improve

22. Research studies have shown that employees who are strongly interested in achievement and advancement on the job usually want assignments where the chance of success is _____, and desire _____ supervisory evaluation of their performance.
    A. low; frequent
    B. high; general
    C. high; infrequent
    D. moderate; specific

23. Of the following, a function of the supervisor that concerns itself with the process of determining a course of action from alternatives is USUALLY referred to as
    A. decentralization
    B. planning
    C. controlling
    D. input

24. Favorable working conditions are an important variable in producing an effective work unit.
    Which of the following would be LEAST conducive in providing a favorable work situation?
    A. Applying a job enrichment program to a routine clerical position
    B. Setting practical goals for the work unit which are consistent with the overall objective of the agency
    C. Assigning individuals to positions which require a higher level of educational achievement than that which they possess
    D. Establishing a communications system which distributes information and provides feedback to all organizational levels

25. Ever supervisor within an organization should know to whom he reports and who reports to him.
Within the organization, this will MOST likely insure
    A. unity of command
    B. confidentiality of sensitive issues
    C. excellent morale
    D. the elimination of the grapevine

25.____

KEY (CORRECT ANSWERS)

1.	A		11.	B
2.	A		12.	A
3.	C		13.	D
4.	D		14.	D
5.	B		15.	C
6.	C		16.	A
7.	C		17.	D
8.	B		18.	A
9.	C		19.	B
10.	D		20.	A

21. C
22. D
23. B
24. C
25. A

TEST 3

DIRECTIONS: Each question or incomplete statement is followed by several suggested answers or completions. Select the one that BEST answers the question or completes the statement. *PRINT THE LETTER OF THE CORRECT ANSWER IN THE SPACE AT THE RIGHT.*

1. In trying to improve the motivation of his subordinates, a supervisor can achieve the BEST results by taking action based upon the assumption that *most* employees
    A. have an inherent dislike of work
    B. wish to be closely directed
    C. are more interested in security than in assuming responsibility
    D. will exercise self-direction without coercion

    1.____

2. Supervisors in public departments have many functions.
   Of the following, the function which is LEAST appropriate for a supervisor is to
    A. serve as a deputy for the administrator within his own unit
    B. determine needs within his unit and plan programs to meet these needs
    C. supervise, train, and evaluate all personnel assigned to his unit
    D. initiate and carry out fundraising projects, such as bazaars and carnivals, to buy needed equipment

    2.____

3. When there are conflicts or tensions between top management and lower-level employees in any public department, the supervisor should FIRSTS attempt to
    A. represent and enforce the management point of view
    B. act as the representative of the workers to get their ideas across to management
    C. serve as a two-way spokesman, trying to interpret each side to the other
    D. remain neutral, but keep informed of changes in the situation

    3.____

4. A probationary period for new employees is usually provided in public agencies.
   The MAJOR purpose of such a period is usually to
    A. allow a determination of employee's suitability for the position
    B. obtain evidence as to employee's ability to perform in a higher position
    C. conform to requirement that ethnic hiring goals be met for all positions
    D. train the new employee in the duties of the position

    4.____

5. An effective program of orientation for new employees usually includes all of the following EXCEPT
    A. having the supervisor introduce the new employee to his job, outlining his responsibilities and how to carry them out
    B. permitting the new worker to tour the facility or department, so he can observe all parts of it in action
    C. scheduling meetings for new employees, at which the job requirements are explained to them and they are given personnel manuals
    D. testing the new worker on his skills, and sending him to a centralized in-service workshop

    5.____

6. In-service training is an important responsibility of supervisors. The MAJOR reason for such training is to
   A. avoid future grievance procedures, because employees might say they were not prepared to carry out their jobs
   B. maximize the effectiveness of the department by helping each employee perform at his full potential
   C. satisfy inspection teams from central headquarters of the department
   D. help prevent disagreements with members of the community

7. There are many forms of useful in-service training.
   Of the following, the training method which is NOT an appropriate technique for leadership development is to
   A. provide special workshops or clinics in activity skills
   B. conduct pre-season institutes to familiarize new workers with the program of the department and with their roles
   C. schedule team meetings for problem-solving, including both supervisors and leaders
   D. have the leader rate himself on an evaluation form periodically

8. Of the following techniques of evaluating work training programs, the one that is BEST is to
   A. pass out a carefully designed questionnaire to the trainees at the completion of the program
   B. test the knowledge that trainees have both at the beginning of training and at its completion
   C. interview the trainees at the completion of the program
   D. evaluate performance before and after training for both a control group and an experimental group

9. Assume that a new supervisor is having difficulty making his instructions to subordinates clearly understood.
   The one of the following which is the FIRST step he should take in dealing with this problem is to
   A. set up a training workshop in communication skills
   B. determine the extent and nature of the communication gap
   C. repeat both verbal and written instructions several times
   D. simplify his written and spoken vocabulary

10. Discipline of employees is usually a supervisor's responsibility. There may be several useful forms of disciplinary action in public employment.
    Of the following, the form that is LEAST appropriate is the
    A. written reprimand or warning
    B. involuntary transfer to another work setting
    C. demotion or suspension
    D. assignment of added hours of work each week

11. Of the following, the MOST effective means of dealing with employee disciplinary problems is to
    A. give personality tests to individuals to identify their psychological problems
    B. distribute and discuss a policy manual containing exact rules governing employee behavior
    C. establish a single, clear penalty to be imposed for all wrongdoing irrespective of degree
    D. have supervisors get to know employees well through social mingling

12. A recently developed technique for appraising work performance is to have the supervisor record on a continual basis all significant incidents in each subordinate's behavior that indicate unsuccessful action and those that indicate poor behavior.
    Of the following, a major DISADVANTAGE of this method of performance appraisal is that it
    A. often leads to overly close supervision
    B. results in competition among those subordinates being evaluated
    C. tends to result in superficial judgments
    D. lacks objectivity for evaluating performance

13. Assume that you are a supervisor and have observed the performance of an employee during a period of time. You have concluded that his performance needs improvement.
    In order to approve his performance, it would, therefore, be BEST for you to
    A. note your findings in the employee's personnel folder so that his behavior is a matter of record
    B. report the findings to the personnel officer so he can take prompt action
    C. schedule a problem-solving conference with the employee
    D. recommend his transfer to simpler duties

14. When an employee's absences or latenesses seem to be nearing excessiveness, the supervisor should speak with him to find out what the problem is.
    Of the following, if such a discussion produces no reasonable explanation, the discussion usually BEST serves to
    A. affirm clearly the supervisor's adherence to proper policy
    B. alert other employees that such behavior is unacceptable
    C. demonstrate that the supervisor truly represents higher management
    D. notify the employee that his behavior is being observed and evaluated

15. Assume that an employee willfully and recklessly violates an important agency regulation. The nature of the violation is of such magnitude that it demands immediate action, but the facts of the case are not entirely clear. Further assume that the supervisor is free to make any of the following recommendations.

The MOST appropriate action for the supervisor to take is to recommend that the employee be
A. discharged   B. suspended   C. forced to resign   D. transferred

16. Although employees' titles may be identical, each position in that title may be considerably different.
Of the following, a supervisor should carefully assign each employee to a specific position based PRIMARILY on the employee's
A. capability   B. experience   C. education   D. seniority

16._____

17. The one of the following situations where it is MOST appropriate to transfer an employee to a *similar* assignment is one in which the employee
A. lacks motivation and interest
B. experiences a personality conflict with his supervisor
C. is negligent in the performance of his duties
D. lacks capacity or ability to perform assigned tasks

17._____

18. The one of the following which is LEAST likely to be affected by improvement in the morale of personnel is employee
A. skill   B. absenteeism   C. turnover   D. job satisfaction

18._____

19. The one of the following situations in which it is LEAST appropriate for a supervisor to delegate authority to subordinates is where the supervisor
A. lacks confidence in his own abilities to perform certain work
B. is overburdened and cannot handle all his responsibilities
C. refers all disciplinary problems to his subordinate
D. has to deal with an emergency or crisis

19._____

20. Of the following, the BEST attitude toward the use of volunteers in programs is that volunteers should be
A. discouraged, since they cannot be depended upon to show up regularly
B. employed as a last resort when paid personnel are unavailable
C. seen as an appropriate means of providing leadership, when effectively recruited and supervised
D. eliminated to raise the professionalism of personnel

20._____

21. A supervisor finds that he is spending too much time on routine tasks, and not enough time on coordinating the work of his employees.
It would be MOST advisable for this supervisor to
A. delegate the task of work coordination to a capable subordinate
B. eliminate some of the routine tasks that the unit is required to perform
C. assign some of the routine tasks to his subordinates
D. postpone the performance of routine tasks until he has achieved proper coordination of his employees' work

21._____

22. Of the following, the MOST important reason for having an office manual in looseleaf form rather than in permanent binding is that the looseleaf form
    A. facilitates the addition of new material and the removal of obsolete material
    B. permits several people to use different sections of the manual at the same time
    C. is less expensive to prepare than permanent binding
    D. is more durable than permanent binding

23. In his first discussion with a newly appointed employee, the LEAST important of the following topics for a supervisor of a unit to include is the
    A. duties the subordinate is expected to perform on the job
    B. functions of the unit
    C. methods of determining standards of performance
    D. nature and duration of the training the subordinate will receive on the job

24. A supervisor has just been told by a subordinate, Mr. Jones, that another employee, Mr. Smith, deliberately disobeyed an important rule of the department by taking home some confidential departmental material.
    Of the following courses of action, it would be MOST advisable for the supervisor FIRST to
    A. discuss the matter privately, with both Mr. Jones and Mr. Smith at the same time
    B. call a meeting of the entire staff and discuss the matter generally without mentioning any employee by name
    C. arrange to supervise Mr. Smith's activities more closely
    D. discuss the matter privately with Mr. Smith

25. The one of the following actions which would be MOST efficient and economical for a supervisor to take to minimize the effect of seasonal fluctuations in the workload of his unit is to
    A. increase his permanent staff until it is large enough to handle the work of the busy season
    B. request the purchase of time and labor-saving equipment to be used primarily during the busy season
    C. lower, temporarily, the standards for quality of work performance during peak loads
    D. schedule for the slow season work that it is not essential to perform during the busy season

KEY (CORRECT ANSWERS)

1.	D	11.	B
2.	D	12.	A
3.	C	13.	C
4.	A	14.	D
5.	D	15.	B
6.	B	16.	A
7.	D	17.	B
8.	D	18.	A
9.	B	19.	C
10.	D	20.	C

21. C
22. A
23. C
24. D
25. D

TEST 4

DIRECTIONS: Each question or incomplete statement is followed by several suggested answers or completions. Select the one that BEST answers the question or completes the statement. *PRINT THE LETTER OF THE CORRECT ANSWER IN THE SPACE AT THE RIGHT.*

1. Assume that, while instructing a worker on a new procedure, the instructor asks, at frequent intervals, whether there are any questions.
   His asking for questions is a
   A. *good practice*, because it affords the worker an opportunity to participate actively in the lesson
   B. *good practice*, because it may reveal points that are not understood by the worker
   C. *poor practice*, because workers generally find it embarrassing to ask questions
   D. *poor practice*, because it may result in wasting time on irrelevant matters

2. Any person thoroughly familiar with the specific steps in a particular type of work is well-qualified to serve as a training course instructor in the work.
   This statement is *erroneous* CHIEFLY because
   A. a qualified instructor cannot be expected to have detailed information about many specific fields
   B. a person who knows a field thoroughly may not be good at passing his knowledge along to others
   C. it is practically impossible for any instructor to be acquainted with all the specific steps in a particular type of work
   D. what is true of one type of work is not necessarily true of other types of work

3. Of the following traits, the one that is LEAST essential for the "ideal" supervisor is that she
   A. be consistent in her interpretation of the rules and policies of the agency for which she works
   B. is able to judge a person's ability at her first meeting with that person
   C. know her own job thoroughly
   D. appreciate and acknowledge honest effort and above-average work

4. The one of the following which is generally the basic reason for using standard procedure is to
   A. serve as a basis for formulating policies
   B. provide the sequence of steps for handling recurring activities
   C. train new employees in the policies and objectives
   D. facilitate periodic review of standard practices

5. An employee, while working at the bookkeeping machine, accidentally kicks off the holdup alarm system. She notifies the supervisor that she can hear the holdup alarm bell ringing, and requests that the holdup alarm system be reset. After the holdup alarm system has been reset, the supervisor should notify the manager that the alarm
   A. is in proper working order
   B. should be shut off while the employee is working the bookkeeping machine to avoid another such accident
   C. kick-plate should be moved away from the worker's reception window so that it cannot be set off accidentally
   D. should be relocated so that it cannot be heard in the bookkeeping office

6. A supervisor who spends a considerate amount of time correcting subordinates' procedural errors should consider FIRST the possibility of
   A. disciplining those who make errors consistently
   B. instituting refresher training sessions
   C. redesigning work forms
   D. requesting that the requirements for entry-level jobs be changed

7. A supervisor has a subordinate who has been late the past four mornings. Of the following, the MOST important action for the supervisor to take FIRST is to
   A. read the rules concerning lateness to the employee in an authoritative manner
   B. give the subordinate a chance to explain the reason for his lateness
   C. tell the employee he must come in on time the next day
   D. ask the friends of the employee whether they can tell him the reason for the employee's lateness

8. During a conversation, a subordinate tells his supervisor about a family problem. For the supervisor to give EXPLICIT advice to the subordinate would be
   A. *desirable*, primarily because a happy employee is more likely to be productive
   B. *undesirable*, primarily because the supervisor should not allow a subordinate to discuss personal problems
   C. *desirable*, primarily because their personal relations will show a marked improvement
   D. *undesirable*, primarily because a supervisor should not take responsibility for handling a subordinate's personal problem

9. As a supervisor, you have received instructions for a drastic change in the procedure for processing cases. Of the following, the approach which is MOST likely to result in acceptance of the change by your subordinates is for you to
   A. inform all subordinates of the change by written memo so that they will have guidelines to follow
   B. ask your superior to inform the unit members about the change at a staff meeting

5.____

6.____

7.____

8.____

9.____

C. recruit the most experienced employee in the unit to give individual instruction to the other unit members
D. discuss the change and the reasons for it with the staff so that they understand their role in its implementation

10. Of the following, the principle which should GENERALLY guide a supervisor in the training of employees under his supervision is that 10.____
    A. training of employees should be delegated to more experienced employees in the same title
    B. primary emphasis should be placed on training for future assignments
    C. the training process should be a highly individual matter
    D. training efforts should concentrate on employees who have the greatest potential

KEY (CORRECT ANSWERS)

1.	B	6.	B
2.	B	7.	B
3.	B	8.	D
4.	B	9.	D
5.	D	10.	C

EXAMINATION SECTION
TEST 1

DIRECTIONS: Each question or incomplete statement is followed by several suggested answers or completions. Select the one that BEST answers the question or completes the statement. *PRINT THE LETTER OF THE CORRECT ANSWER IN THE SPACE AT THE RIGHT.*

1. Which of the following are covered under the definition of customer service? 1._____
   A. A positive environment set up to efficiently handle customer requests
   B. Infrastructure designed to distribute merchandise in a timely fashion
   C. Employees filling distinct roles to meet customer needs
   D. All of the above

2. An organization that has a clearly established customer service approach can distinguish itself from competitors. This is referred to as the organization's 2._____
   A. customer prioritization   B. service culture
   C. imagineering   D. none of the above

3. The physical space of a hospitality setting is MOST commonly referred to as the 3._____
   A. customer landscape   B. business policy
   C. servicescape   D. arena of service

4. When dealing with a customer, one must be knowledgeable, capable and enthusiastic when delivering products and/or services and it must be done in a manner that satisfies 4._____
   A. both identified and unidentified needs
   B. local and global competition
   C. quality and quantity of goods/services
   D. all demands of the customer

5. Employees at the center learn at their orientation that services are inseparable because service quality and customer satisfaction are largely dependent on which of the following? 5._____
   A. Interactions between employees and customers
   B. Uniform offerings for individuals
   C. Establishing patents for individual services
   D. All of the above

6. An organization with a strong customer service culture 6._____
   A. allows employees to use their own initiative to solve customer problems
   B. has policies that allow employees to easily please customers
   C. provides extensive customer service training for employees
   D. all of the above

7. Which of the following is TRUE of customer contact through electronic mail?
   A. Be sure to use all caps for important aspects of the e-mail
   B. State the purpose of the message clearly
   C. Do not feel the need to respond immediately
   D. Include lengthy descriptions in the body of the e-mail

8. A clerk is speaking to residents at a zoning committee meeting and uses the word "coulda" instead of "could have" in his presentation.
   This is an example of
   A. good enunciation
   B. poor tone
   C. poor enunciation
   D. proper pitch

9. An employee is delivering a presentation to parents about the benefits of children joining summer camps when someone complains that the employee's changing pitch makes it hard to hear what he is saying and that he needs to fix it.
   What does the parent mean by fixing his pitch?
   The employee needs to
   A. keep his voice from going too high or too low
   B. keep his voice from getting too soft or too loud
   C. keep his attitude towards certain subjects in check
   D. make sure his words are clearly spoken and not garbled

10. A clerk recently moved from answering phone calls every day to working face-to-face with residents.
    Which of the following will help her be most successful when transferring from phone to personal communication?
    A. Focus on sharing only positive information
    B. Speak more authoritatively
    C. Maintain a more casual tone and familiarity with residents
    D. Positive communication through eye contact and body language

11. Talking via telephone
    A. is less personal than sending an e-mail message
    B. is a poor way to reach most residents
    C. can allow residents to receive instant feedback
    D. is not popular within public services

12. An employee is in charge of calling local homeowners to tell them about upcoming activities, and more often than not she needs to leave a voicemail.
    Which of the following is the MOST effective way to leave voicemails?
    A. Be courteous
    B. Provide the appropriate information
    C. Contain lengthy details
    D. Both A and B

13. You are dealing with a parent who is upset about a miscommunication related to her child's application for an activity. Which of the following would be LEAST frustrating for the parent to hear from you?
    A. "I don't know. I will do my best."
    B. "Let me see what I can do for you."
    C. "I apologize, but you will have to…"
    D. "Oh, my manager should be able to help you, but he's not in right now."

14. If a part-time assistant employee should need to apologize to customers, which of the following should he NOT do when apologizing?
    A. Apologize right away
    B. Be sincere in his apology
    C. Make the apology personal
    D. Offer an official apology from the department

15. If a clerk's office is looking to improve its processes to increase community satisfaction, feedback received should be each of the following EXCEPT
    A. centered on internal customers
    B. ongoing
    C. available internally to everyone from employees to supervisors
    D. focused on a limited number of indicators

16. A member of the community has identified a flaw in one of the policies regarding town hall meetings. Now that the problem has been identified, all of the following should be steps toward resolving the issue EXCEPT
    A. following up on the problem resolution
    B. making whatever promises are necessary
    C. listening and responding to all complaints
    D. providing the resident with whatever was originally requested

17. When looking to achieve the best results as someone who interacts with the public, one should always strive to represent
    A. the entire organization   B. the customer
    C. the department   D. their direct supervisor

18. Approximately how long does it take a person on hold to become annoyed?
    A. 1 minute   B. 40 seconds   C. 20 seconds   D. 2 minutes

19. If an employee answers the phone and is asked to transfer the call to a co-worker, which of the following would be the MOST appropriate response?
    A. "She isn't in right now, so I'll have to take a message."
    B. "She's still at lunch. Can I take a message?"
    C. "She should be back soon. Could you call back in 15 minutes?"
    D. "Let me transfer you. If she's not in, please leave a message and she will return your call."

20. A public employee has been specifically assigned to deal with public complaints because he is remarkably skilled at dealing with residents. Which of the following mentalities would explain why the employee is so effective at dealing with residents?
    A. They always cave in to whatever demands the residents make
    B. They effectively manage residents' expectations
    C. They always sincerely apologize no matter who is at fault
    D. Both A and C

21. When dealing with a frustrated customer, which of the following practices should an employee avoid?
    A. Immediately offer a solution to their problem
    B. Soothe the customer's frustration first
    C. Remain positive and non-confrontational with the customer
    D. Let the customer vent and feel like they've shared their feelings accurately

22. The town clerk's office in Avondale is highly rated by town residents. When surveyed, residents of Avondale claim that their town clerks always have such great customer service.
    Of the customer service techniques listed below, which one is MOST likely the reason for such high ratings?
    A. When dealing with abusive residents, Avondale clerks always hang up on them
    B. Clerks in Avondale have a readied list of solutions to resident problems, so they are able to offer personalized solutions right away
    C. Avondale clerks always follow up with residents who call or come in
    D. Clerks always look customers in the eye even when they are frustrated and upset

23. If a parent was told there would be space in a day camp for all of her children, and only two of them ended up being placed together, which of the following actions would be PROPER for a parks employee to take?
    A. Offer a sincere apology and attempt to fix the problem
    B. Promise the parent that all her children will be together even if it means dropping other children from the camp
    C. Explain the Parks Department policy regarding camp sign-up and tell the parent to contact a manager for further explanation
    D. Tell the parent she needs to speak to someone with more authority

24. If a person has a hearing impairment, which of the following practical solutions could a clerk have in place to help them?
    A. Reading a description of policy to the person
    B. Write a note to answer a question they have
    C. Read the words communicated by the person's "communication board"
    D. Assist the person in maneuvering through the physical space of the office

25. When dealing with a call, who should end the phone call first?
    A. The person who answered
    B. The person who called
    C. Either one – it doesn't matter
    D. A manager

25._____

KEY (CORRECT ANSWERS)

1. D
2. B
3. C
4. A
5. A

6. D
7. B
8. C
9. A
10. D

11. C
12. D
13. B
14. D
15. A

16. B
17. A
18. C
19. D
20. B

21. A
22. C
23. A
24. B
25. B

TEST 2

DIRECTIONS: Each question or incomplete statement is followed by several suggested answers or completions. Select the one that BEST answers the question or completes the statement. *PRINT THE LETTER OF THE CORRECT ANSWER IN THE SPACE AT THE RIGHT.*

1. Which of the following would be considered acceptable for an office clerk when answering the phone?
   A. Chewing gum
   B. Listening to music
   C. Eating a snack while on mute
   D. Wearing a headset

   1.____

2. Why would asking a caller for their phone number be important?
   A. In case they get disconnected
   B. To show them you are polite and considerate
   C. In case the caller is rude, this way you can call them back
   D. For future instances where calling residents back might make sense

   2.____

3. When rolling out a new program to help train employees in better customer service, the manager starts off by talking about the importance of telephone greetings.
   Why is this so important?
   A. It is the first impression the customer has of the department
   B. It shows the customer that employees are happy
   C. It shows that you are polite
   D. It isn't that important, but the manager thinks it is

   3.____

4. Which of the following is the MOST important aspect of an employee's voice in a telephone call?
   A. Their volume
   B. Their speed
   C. Their tone
   D. All of these aspects are equally important

   4.____

5. A clerk is on the phone with a customer when another customer walks into the building.
   If the clerk must put the caller on hold, what do they need to say or ask?
   A. "Would you like to be put on hold?"
   B. "I apologize for the inconvenience, but please hold."
   C. "Would it be OK if I put you on hold for a moment?"
   D. "I have to let you go. Please call back later."

   5.____

6. When a resident comes into your office for a face-to-face meeting, it is of increased importance that you communicate positively with your
   A. words
   B. body language
   C. tone
   D. none of the above

   6.____

7. A customer calls when employees are at an all-staff meeting. When calling the customer back, a clerk reaches their voicemail.
   Which of the following information is the MOST important to leave?
   A. The date and time
   B. Ask them to call back
   C. The employee's telephone number
   D. Apologize repeatedly for missing their call

8. If an employee is in the middle of a conversation about town hall policy with a co-worker and the phone rings, what should the employee do?
   A. Get caller's information and call back after the conversation is finished
   B. Tell the co-worker to wait until finished with the phone call
   C. Answer the call and put caller on hold until conversation is finished
   D. Answer the call and transfer it to another employee who is not currently busy

9. When dealing with a resident who casually uses vulgar language, it is MOST appropriate for a town employee to
   A. tell the resident to come back when he learns how to speak
   B. converse with the resident using equally coarse language
   C. politely ask the resident to refrain from using vulgar language
   D. make the resident wait longer so he knows it won't be tolerated

10. The mayor's office has recently come under fire for a variety of perceived scandals.
    In this emergency situation, which of the following would NOT be a recommended step in handling the crisis?
    A. Minimizing damage to the office's reputation through whatever means necessary
    B. Taking responsibility and apologizing
    C. Providing constant updates on the situation
    D. Designating one spokesperson to handle the relaying of updates

11. A resident complains that recreation center employees are using bureaucratic or overly technical communication. This type of language is often referred to as
    A. clichés   B. jargon   C. euphemisms   D. legalese

12. Which of the following strategies does an employee need to utilize to convince the public to believe a message that is contrary to their beliefs?
    A. Cognitive dissonance   B. Uses and gratification
    C. Sleeper effect   D. Source credibility

13. When communicating with parents of a summer camp run by the district, which of the following should NOT be a goal of the process?
    A. Motivation   B. Persuasion
    C. Mutual understanding   D. Isolation of the conflict

14. A manager comes up with a new procedure that he believes would improve the claims process that residents need to go through. Some employees agree that the procedure would make sense and others do not. One employee openly criticizes the idea to the manager.
Which of the following actions should the manager take?
He should
    A. meet with the employee for a talk and explain why bypassing his authority is unacceptable
    B. not respond to the critics in order to avoid unnecessary risks
    C. reprimand the employee who went over his head
    D. only implement the procedures that all agreed were good in order to satisfy employees

14._____

15. The county clerk's office is working on improving its employees' professionalism.
If employees are attempting to maintain a professional demeanor, what should they NOT do after making a mistake?
    A. Work to do better at the next opportunity
    B. Move on
    C. Accept responsibility
    D. Explain or rationalize the error

15._____

16. According to most recent surveys, data reveals that most white-collar workers
    A. have about a 25 percent efficiency rate when listening
    B. lose only about 25 percent efficiency when listening
    C. never take listening for granted
    D. learn to listen effectively since hearing is the important active learned process

16._____

17. Which of the following are NOT one of the four phases of listening to a customer?
    A. Hearing   B. Translating   C. Responding   D. Comprehending

17._____

18. Which of the following societal factors might impact a resident/employee interaction?
    A. Increased efficiency in technology
    B. Globalization of the economy
    C. More people between the ages of 16-24 entering the workplace
    D. Geopolitical changes

18._____

19. If a resident comes in confused about a policy change, which of the following approaches should an employee take to handle the situation?
    A. Communicate negatively when they need to
    B. Avoid gestures such as smiling or looking at customers when speaking to them
    C. Recognize how they tend to communicate and adjust accordingly if the customer is still showing signs of confusion
    D. Understand that many people are doubtful of good customer service

19._____

20. In order to avoid negative public perception, which of the following "finger pointing" words/phrases should be avoided when interacting with the public?
    A. Let me   B. You   C. Why   D. Yes

21. In an effort to improve government/resident relations, the mayor wants to roll out a new PR format that stresses public communication.
    Which of the following strategies should NOT be suggested as part of the PR campaign?
    A. Plan the message
    B. Greet residents warmly
    C. Listen carefully and respond appropriately
    D. Let the residents initiate conversations

22. A resident complains that the department does not always treat the local residents as people.
    Of the following, which would be the BEST strategy for resolving this issue?
    A. Accept responsibility and offer specific assistance
    B. Blame the customer when necessary
    C. Provide policies as reasons for actions
    D. None of the above

23. When providing feedback to residents, which of the following strategies is NOT effective?
    A. Remain emotional when providing feedback
    B. Confirm residents' meaning before offering feedback
    C. Ensure the feedback is appropriate to the original message
    D. Avoid extreme criticism or negative language

24. An employee at City Hall receives special treatment from his manager. This causes the employee to feel empowered, which then leads to him abusing authority and power.
    Which of the following would MOST likely happen if this behavior is allowed to continue?
    A. Other employees would begin to feel empowered
    B. Co-workers would work harder to demonstrate their commitment
    C. Residents would begin to work with the empowered employee because he would be able to get things done
    D. The rest of the department would start to feel resentment and frustration, and might potentially retaliate

25. If a town clerk works well with customers on the phone but struggles with face-to-face interactions, which of the following might BEST explain the problem?
    A. The actual words the clerk uses   B. Facial and other body cues
    C. Vocal cues   D. Both A and C

KEY (CORRECT ANSWERS)

1.	D	11.	B
2.	A	12.	A
3.	A	13.	D
4.	D	14.	A
5.	C	15.	D
6.	B	16.	A
7.	C	17.	B
8.	B	18.	C
9.	C	19.	C
10.	A	20.	B

21. D
22. A
23. A
24. D
25. B

TEST 3

DIRECTIONS: Each question or incomplete statement is followed by several suggested answers or completions. Select the one that BEST answers the question or completes the statement. *PRINT THE LETTER OF THE CORRECT ANSWER IN THE SPACE AT THE RIGHT.*

1. If an employee's body position is causing customers to feel she is projecting a mood/attitude that she isn't actually expressing, what does the employee need to work on improving?
    A. Pitch
    B. Articulation
    C. Posture
    D. Inflection

    1.____

2. A newly hired assistant notices that everyone in his department has received a new computer system except for him.
   What should he do?
    A. Assume this is a mistake and speak to his manager
    B. Complain to H.R.
    C. Quit
    D. Confront his manager regarding his unfair treatment

    2.____

3. A team leader in your department notices that ample amounts of department-labeled property have come up missing in recent weeks. The leader notices a fellow supervisor putting stationery and other equipment into a personal bag on a few different occasions and believes this person is responsible.
   What is the LEAST effective response to the situation?
    A. Gather more evidence to catch the person in the act
    B. Do nothing – if guilty, someone else will likely catch the colleague
    C. Privately ask other colleagues if they've noticed anything suspicious recently
    D. Inform a supervisor higher up in the organization that this person is a potential suspect

    3.____

4. Near the end of the work day, an official advisor accidentally sends an e-mail containing confidential information to the wrong person.
   Which of the following would be the BEST thing for the advisor to do?
    A. Overlook the error. Send the e-mail to the correct person and leave things as they are.
    B. Find a senior advisor and explain the mistake and have them deal with the problem
    C. Leave the office and deal with any fallout tomorrow
    D. Immediately send a follow-up e-mail to the "wrong" person explaining the mistake. Then send the e-mail to the correct person.

    4.____

5. If an employee is engaged with a customer and no one else is around when the phone rings, what is the PROPER step to take in this situation?
   A. Let the phone ring and continue to work with the customer in person
   B. Take the call and address the caller's issue, then hang up and come back to the customer
   C. Ask the customer to answer the phone while trying to resolve their issue.
   D. Tell the customer "excuse me" while answering the phone, then put the caller on hold while going back to the customer

5.____

6. According to many national retailer surveys, what do consumers remember the MOST about their customer service experience?
   A. The cost of the merchandise/experience
   B. The demeanor of the employee who engaged them
   C. The cleanliness of the office/area
   D. How nice the employees were

6.____

7. When attempting to help a resident make a decision about programs offered by your agency, it is important to remember that the majority of purchasing decisions consumers make are based upon
   A. what they think
   B. a potential free gift
   C. how they feel
   D. all of the above

7.____

8. In an effort to improve procedures in your department, a memo has been sent to employees. In it, one highlighted section focuses on the importance of avoiding closed-ended questions/comments.
   Following the advice of the memo, which question/comment should an employee avoid stating to a resident?
   A. "Can I help you?"
   B. "What is it you would like to see accomplished?"
   C. "So the challenges you've faced so far are..."
   D. "How would you like to see that improved?"

8.____

9. Numerous surveys indicate that consumers would actually pay more for
   A. self-checkout machines
   B. free product/demonstration giveaways
   C. more streamlined customer service
   D. apps using customer-service bots

9.____

10. Which of the following is an example of a proper "Activation Greeting"?
    A. "My name is _____. Let me tell you about our programs."
    B. "How many are there in your group?"
    C. "Hi! Welcome to _____."
    D. Both A and C

10.____

11. When interacting with members of the public, which of the following is the MOST important thing to do?
    A. Ask them to pay for services up front
    B. Smile at them
    C. Learn their name and call them by it
    D. Ask questions

12. Which of the following pieces of advice would help a clerk the MOST when working with the public?
    A. Pay attention to needs of others and offer only general solutions
    B. Hear what others are saying but do not take their comments to heart
    C. Focus on efficiency of service over quality of service
    D. Clearly understand the motives and needs of others

13. A member of the community complains that counselors at her child's camp do not listen to what she is telling them.
    Which technique listed below would improve understanding between the two parties?
    A. Reflective listening
    B. Narrow selections
    C. Reflective thinking
    D. Valid suggestions

14. When dealing with elderly residents, which of the following facts should be considered by a public official?
    A. They expect to be treated with courtesy and respect
    B. Expect them to avoid eye contact
    C. They prefer the telephone to personal contact
    D. They expect text and e-mail over face-to-face communication

15. If you are hired as a camp counselor for younger residents, it is important to remember all of the following about their behavior EXCEPT that they
    A. value technology
    B. are used to multitasking and access to instant information
    C. make less eye contact
    D. prefer more formal interactions

16. If one is trying to improve morale regarding customer/worker relations, which of the following is NOT a recommended thing to do?
    A. Publicly embarrass customers who are rude to the office employees
    B. Greet the customer with "Good Morning"
    C. Politely ask customers who cut in line to wait until it is their turn
    D. Thank customers for doing business with you

17. When hired by a public office, which of the following would be part of the newly hired employee's performance code?
    A. Report on time in a calm and controlled manner
    B. Present oneself in a neat and clean way
    C. Treat co-workers and residents with dignity and respect
    D. All of the above

18. If an employee sometimes "bends the rules" to honor a request from a customer, what service concept would explain this action?
    A. Motivated marketing strategy
    B. Power selling philosophy
    C. Employee empowerment
    D. Selling out for the customer

19. A Parks and Recreation worker is attempting to improve relations with the groups who sign up for his arts and crafts program.
    He should remember all of the following "Customer Service Rules" EXCEPT
    A. Customer service has a large effect on customer satisfaction
    B. Modern consumers are already more satisfied with customer service today than ever before
    C. Modern consumers have many different mechanisms by which to complain
    D. Feeling empowered as an employee usually leads to higher customer satisfaction

20. A marketing executive employee wishes to emphasize customer loyalty. Which of the following marketing strategies should the employee focus on when working with customers?
    A. Relationship marketing
    B. Undercover marketing
    C. Diversity marketing
    D. Transactional marketing

21. Why would a campaign manager for an elected official be interested in conducting a mail survey over other methods of surveying?
    It would
    A. avoid non-response problems
    B. speed up the process by which surveys are returned to them
    C. avoid participation by incorrect respondents
    D. enable the completion of the survey at a convenient time

22. At the end of each session, a counselor takes it upon herself to conduct research on the effectiveness of the program. She is worried that respondents won't be truthful, so she decides that the BEST way to avoid bias would be to conduct a(n) _____ survey.
    A. personal
    B. telephone
    C. internet
    D. observational

23. A resident walks into the office and submits an application. When she is given additional forms to complete, she grumbles about "bureaucratic red tape" and how it's slowing down her application approval.
    How should an employee handle this situation?
    A. Be patient with the resident but do not explain the reason for the forms
    B. Tell the resident why the additional forms are necessary
    C. Suggest that the resident take it up with the manager if she wants the policy changed
    D. Say that the application will not be processed until ALL forms are completed

24. An employee's next-door neighbor has been hired as summer help, which the employee knows about because he has to type a confidential letter from the director to human resources about the hire. The neighbor does not yet know of the hiring decision, and the employee will see the neighbor later that day. Which one of the following should the employee do?   24._____
    A. Say nothing and wait for the offer to become official
    B. Congratulate the neighbor confidentially
    C. Inform a handful of people including the neighbor's close friends
    D. None of the above

25. A child with vision impairment wants to join a summer day camp and is denied access because the camp focuses on games and activities in which sight is required. If the parent comes in and complains to you, which of the following actions should you take and why?   25._____
    A. Modify the camp so the child can join because it is bad publicity to deny a child with a disability
    B. Offer another camp that does not focus on so many "sight-based" activities at a reduced rate so the parent and child do not feel left out
    C. Enroll the child and ensure they are allowed to participate in a meaningful way, because it's against the law to prevent the child from signing up
    D. Tell the parent they can talk to a supervisor because you have no authority to change the decision

---

KEY (CORRECT ANSWERS)

1.	C		11.	B
2.	A		12.	D
3.	B		13.	A
4.	D		14.	A
5.	D		15.	D
6.	B		16.	A
7.	C		17.	D
8.	A		18.	C
9.	C		19.	B
10.	C		20.	A

21. D
22. C
23. B
24. A
25. C

TEST 4

DIRECTIONS: Each question or incomplete statement is followed by several suggested answers or completions. Select the one that BEST answers the question or completes the statement. *PRINT THE LETTER OF THE CORRECT ANSWER IN THE SPACE AT THE RIGHT.*

1. If a customer tells an employee they need to work on having open body language, which of the following would be an example?
   A. Fiddling
   B. Minimal eye contact
   C. Folded arms
   D. Frequent hand gestures

   1.____

2. As a phone operator for the bureau director's office, it is important that you make the constituents feel as though you are actively listening to their concerns.
   What is the MOST effective way to demonstrate this?
   A. Use affirmation with words like "ok", "yes" and "I understand"
   B. Interrupt with your own thoughts
   C. Ask numerous closed questions
   D. Talk over the constituent

   2.____

3. When a resident walks up to a clerk's desk, which of the following is the BEST way to greet them?
   A. Wave
   B. Ask them what they need
   C. Welcome them and ask how they can be helped
   D. Ignore them until finished with the current task

   3.____

4. When a customer complains through e-mail, an office clerk should
   A. forward the e-mail to a supervisor
   B. reply right away with a potential solution
   C. share the complaint via the office's official Twitter handle
   D. reply right away with a hurried answer

   4.____

5. Interacting with the public is a constant back and forth where feedback is essential to improving service.
   Which of the following methods would be BEST to obtain feedback from the public?
   A. Cold calling
   B. Tweeting
   C. Survey via website
   D. Ask the staff what they think

   5.____

6. If residents continually complain that clerks do not truly understand what they are trying to tell them, which of the following practices might help improve this communication barrier?
   A. Paraphrasing
   B. Encoding
   C. Rapport building
   D. Decoding

   6.____

7. A customer complains to an employee and demands to see a supervisor. The employee is not sure to who to direct this angry customer.
Which of the following methods of illustrating hierarchy of the company would help the employee out?
   A. Diagramming
   B. Negotiation
   C. Brainstorming
   D. Organizational charts

7.____

8. A village clerk and a resident have a strong disagreement about how an office policy applies to their situation. A co-worker is asked to weigh in on the situation.
How should the co-worker handle the situation?
   A. Take the employee's side since they have to work side by side
   B. Try to help both parties walk away feeling like they got what they wanted
   C. Take the resident's side since the office cannot afford bad publicity
   D. Have a supervisor intervene – it's better to pass responsibility onto someone in power

8.____

9. A parent accuses your department of making generalizations about their child based on the group to which they belong.
Which of the following unfair, but common, ideas is the department being accused of?
   A. Racism
   B. Stereotyping
   C. Confirmation bias
   D. Rationale judgment

9.____

10. When a resident calls a government office, they expect the phone to be picked up by the _____ ring otherwise they feel as though their call is unimportant.
    A. 1st
    B. 4th
    C. 3rd
    D. 7th

10.____

11. When working directly with a consumer on the phone or in person, which of the following would be considered inappropriate?
    A. Eating, drinking or chewing gum
    B. Speaking slowly and enunciating clearly
    C. Asking permission to put someone on hold
    D. Wearing a headset

11.____

12. Someone calls village hall and is extremely upset by a policy change enacted in the last board meeting. They demand an explanation that the clerk does not have.
As the clerk tries to find the answer, how often should she update the angry caller on the status of the complaint (even if the clerk has no answer)?
    A. 2-3 minutes
    B. 35 seconds
    C. 1 minute
    D. Do not update them until an answer has been found

12.____

13. A resident is irate over how a co-worker of yours handled his claim process and now you have to handle his appeal. Throughout the process of filling out the necessary paperwork, this resident continues to not only berate the co-worker, but also starts complaining about how slow you are.
In this stressful situation, why is it important to stay calm and not let the resident get to you?
    A. They could be having a bad day and your anger may make the situation worse
    B. You need to show the resident you are willing to take the time necessary to resolve his or her problem
    C. They might be violent and could end up hurting you
    D. Both A and B

13.____

14. An employee is calling residents to thank them for volunteering for a food drive. As the employee moves through his list, he accidentally dials the wrong number, and a person on the other line answers.
What should the employee do?
    A. Apologize to the person for calling the wrong number
    B. Thank the person anyway
    C. Hang up before the person says anything else
    D. Try to sign the person up for the next food drive

14.____

15. Which of the following questions tell the customer that the employee wants to ensure that every need has been met before the interaction is over?
    A. "You've said everything you need to say, right?"
    B. "Is there anything else I can help you with?"
    C. "How can I help you today?"
    D. "Would you like me to transfer you to someone else?"

15.____

16. An elderly resident calls your department, but was trying to reach the Health and Sanitation Department. What should you do?
    A. Be polite
    B. Hastily transfer the person to the correct department
    C. Try to determine who they need to speak to and transfer them to that person directly if possible
    D. Both A and C

16.____

17. Which of the following would NOT be considered an example of good customer service?
    A. A parent waits three minutes to pick up their child from an after-school activity
    B. A clearly defined resolution process is in place for residents who have disagreements with public officials
    C. There is no line at the DMV, and a person waits 10 minutes before being serviced
    D. The park's pools briefly close at noon and 4 p.m. so they can be skimmed and checked for debris

17.____

18. A resident is angry about a zoning issue that prevents him from adding on to his garage.
    When dealing with this customer, which of the following should an employee NOT do?
    A. Acknowledge their emotion
    B. Ask questions
    C. Avoid escalating the argument
    D. Agree that the code is silly

18.____

19. A resident comes into the office where you work and complains that he was screened out of a job because of a vision impairment. He asks if this is legal and what he should do.
    You tell him it is not against the Americans With Disabilities Act if the employer screens him because
    A. clients prefer not to be served by the disabled
    B. a business cannot make a reasonable accommodation to work tasks for a specific disability
    C. co-workers dislike working with the disabled
    D. none of the above; ADA prevents any kind of "screening out" of disabled persons

19.____

20. During holidays and special events, the school office can sometimes be short-staffed, which requires all employees to know the different roles within the office. Some parents do not like when certain staff members act as the receptionist and those staff members do not like being the receptionist.
    Since both sides do not like the employees in that role, the employees should
    A. learn the receptionist's job and fill in when needed, but tell the principal that they, and parents, would prefer that they work in a different area
    B. tell the principal they don't want to work as a receptionist and ask to be excused from that role
    C. learn the receptionist's job, but when asked to fill in ask someone else to do it
    D. ask the principal to excuse then from the training, and explain that other employees who the parents like more could fill in for them

20.____

21. In an attempt to promote the recreation center in a positive light, which of the following advertising strategies would be MOST credible to town residents?
    A. Employees telling people how great the recreation center environment is
    B. Have local celebrities endorse the recreation center as the place to be
    C. Use current satisfied customers by having them "spread the word" about the recreation center
    D. Offer incredible discounts to the first 25 new customers to sign up

21.____

22. When a clerk is tasked with setting up a Town Hall meeting, all of the following are important EXCEPT
    A. spreading the word
    B. having an audience-selected moderator
    C. setting and following a schedule
    D. keeping things moving

22.____

23. A librarian works in the computer lab and a patron comes to her and says, "My flash drive is full. I need to save the document I just created. Where can I get a new flash drive?"
How should the librarian respond?
    A. Offer to help the patron e-mail the document to himself and then show him how to do it
    B. Ask the patron what he needs to save and then save it to a "Google Document" for them
    C. Offer him the use of a library-owned flash drive on the promise that he will bring it back
    D. Direct him to the nearest computer/retail store to purchase the flash drive

23._____

24. If people call for a Town Hall meeting, which of the following would NOT be a good reason to hold one?
    A. To voice a common concern shared by members of the community
    B. To present a new proposal that impacts the public
    C. To settle a dispute between rival advisors at City Hall
    D. To collect feedback in response to a new rule or policy implementation

24._____

25. Of the following Town Hall meeting pitfalls, which would MOST leave residents feeling as though they wasted their time?
    A. Not participative or interactive
    B. Poorly designed PowerPoint or on-screen presentation
    C. Poor time management
    D. Meaningless or irrelevant content

25._____

KEY (CORRECT ANSWERS)

1.	D	11.	A
2.	A	12.	C
3.	C	13.	D
4.	B	14.	A
5.	C	15.	B
6.	A	16.	D
7.	D	17.	C
8.	B	18.	D
9.	B	19.	B
10.	C	20.	A

21. C
22. B
23. A
24. C
25. D

EXAMINATION SECTION
TEST 1

DIRECTIONS: Each question or incomplete statement is followed by several suggested answers or completions. Select the one that BEST answers the question or completes the statement. *PRINT THE LETTER OF THE CORRECT ANSWER IN THE SPACE AT THE RIGHT.*

1. A group member who starts out at the same level as other group members and is able to move into a leadership position within that group would be described as what kind of a leader?
   A. Autocratic   B. Democratic   C. Emergent   D. Informal

   1._____

2. Your boss is only effective as the leader of your department when you and your coworkers are motivated experts on the topic at hand. If any of you do not really have expertise in a given field, his leadership falters somewhat. What type of leader is your boss?
   A. Laissez-faire   B. Technical   C. Democratic   D. Autocratic

   2._____

3. If a leader is in charge of an inexperienced group that does not have the appropriate information and proficiency to successfully complete a task, which of the following approaches should the leader use in order for success to follow within the group?
   A. Yelling   B. Delegating   C. Participating   D. Selling

   3._____

4. If you are a democratic leader, which of the following styles will be reflective of your leadership technique?
   A. Participating   B. Telling   C. Yelling   D. Delegating

   4._____

5. In producing equality in group member participation, which of the following should a leader NOT do?
   A. Make a statement or ask a question after each person in the group has said something
   B. Avoid taking a position during disagreements
   C. Limit comments to specific individuals within the group
   D. Control dominating speakers

   5._____

6. Social capital is BEST defined as
   A. social connections that help us make more money
   B. social connections that improve our lives
   C. a type of connection that experts believe is becoming more common in Europe than the United States.
   D. none of the above

   6._____

7. Communication is not simply sending a message. It is creating true
   A. connectivity   B. understanding
   C. empathy   D. power

   7._____

8. Of the following, which is NOT a part of the speech communication process?
   A. Feedback
   B. Central idea
   C. Interference
   D. Ethics

9. You are leading a meeting and afterwards your colleagues tell you they didn't quite understand what you were communicating verbally and nonverbally to them. Which part of the communication process do you need to work on?
   A. Channel
   B. Main idea
   C. Message
   D. Specific purpose

10. If nonverbal messages contradict verbal symbols, you are sending what kind of message to your public?
    A. Clear
    B. Mixed
    C. Controversial
    D. Negative

11. Which of the following would a public speaker use to deliver verbal symbols?
    A. Words
    B. Gestures
    C. Tone
    D. Facial expression

12. You are in the process of taking a course on interacting with the public. Your instructor starts talking about "the pathway" used to transmit a message. He explains that "the pathway" is better known as a
    A. link
    B. loop
    C. transmitter
    D. channel

13. You finish an informational meeting with members of a community concerning a new park that will be built nearby. Afterwards, you are seeking feedback from them. Which of the following would NOT be a form of helpful feedback to you?
    A. Listeners raise their hands to point out a mistake
    B. Videotape the presentation
    C. Have colleagues and/or friends critique your presentation
    D. Hand out evaluation forms to listeners and have them fill it out after the presentation

14. Many public speaking experts have often repeated the famous quote, "A yawn is a silent _____," which references the quality of engagement within a presentation.
    A. rudeness
    B. insult
    C. shout
    D. protest

15. If a child is running around during your speech and making a lot of noise, what type of interference would that be?
    A. Situational
    B. External
    C. Internal
    D. Intentional

16. According to multiple recent surveys, of the five biggest mistakes that speakers make during a presentation, which one is the WORST?
    A. Being poorly prepared
    B. Trying to cover too much in one speech
    C. Failing to tailor a speech to the needs and interests of the audience
    D. Being boring

17. One of your colleagues has been asked to lead a meeting, and she confides in you that she suffers from excessive stage fright. Which of the following areas should you advise her to focus on to prevent her fear?
    A. Preparation
    B. Self-confidence
    C. Experience
    D. Sense of humor

17.____

18. When interacting with the public, which of the following elements should you NEVER imagine before engaging in public speaking?
    A. Effective delivery
    B. Nervousness
    C. Possibility of failure
    D. Success

18.____

19. A spokesperson is giving a speech to community members and you are evaluating him. You notice he tends to focus too much on himself and not enough on his audience. What is one piece of advice you can give him so he can shift his focus more to his audience?
    A. Change his amount of eye contact
    B. Work on facial expressions
    C. Alter his style of speaking
    D. All of the above

19.____

20. Most experts agree that the best way to eliminate excess energy would be to do all of the following EXCEPT
    A. using visual aids
    B. gripping the lectern
    C. walking to the right and left occasionally
    D. making gestures

20.____

21. A woman has lived in Newville her whole life. Recently, the Newville public works department made a policy change that angered her since it completely rearranged her schedule. She calls you on the phone and displays her displeasure with your department's recent policy change. What is the FIRST response you should have toward her?
    A. Interrupt her to say you cannot discuss the situation until she calms down
    B. Apologize to her that she has been negatively affected by the public works department
    C. Listen to her and demonstrate comprehension of her situation and why she was upset by your department's action
    D. Give her a detailed explanation of the reasons for the policy change

21.____

22. Which of the following is generally TRUE regarding public opinion?
    A. It is hard to move people toward a strong opinion on anything
    B. It is easy to move people toward a strong opinion on anything
    C. Most public relations are devoted to repairing negative public opinion about individuals
    D. It is easier than previously thought to move people away from an opinion they hold

22.____

23. Influencing a community member's attitude really comes down to which of the following?
    A. Journalism
    B. Public relations
    C. Social psychology
    D. Social action groups

23.____

4 (#1)

24. If you attend a town hall meeting in which community members will bring up issues that require you to explain why your organization made the decisions it made, you will need to persuade them using evidence that is virtually indisputable. Which type of evidence should you stick to when explaining answers to the public?
    A. Facts
    B. Personal experience
    C. Emotions
    D. Using what appeals to the target public

24._____

25. In the last decade, especially after all the organizational and governmental scandals, public institutions must do which of the following in order to be successful?
    A. Work hard to earn and sustain favorable public opinion
    B. Trust the instincts expressed by the general public
    C. Be cognizant of the media's power
    D. Place the needs of the executives ahead of the needs of the public and other constituents

25._____

KEY (CORRECT ANSWERS)

1.	C		11.	A
2.	A		12.	D
3.	B		13.	A
4.	D		14.	C
5.	A		15.	B
6.	B		16.	C
7.	B		17.	A
8.	D		18.	B
9.	C		19.	D
10.	B		20.	B

21. C
22. D
23. B
24. A
25. A

TEST 2

DIRECTIONS: Each question or incomplete statement is followed by several suggested answers or completions. Select the one that BEST answers the question or completes the statement. *PRINT THE LETTER OF THE CORRECT ANSWER IN THE SPACE AT THE RIGHT.*

1. Unique attributes of the Internet that people can enjoy include all of the following EXCEPT
    A. immediacy
    B. low cost
    C. pervasiveness
    D. value for building one-to-one human relationships

    1.____

2. Which of the following is a reason that social media can be more effective than traditional means of advertising and communication?
    A. When someone mentions your brand in social media, there is much more potential for other people to notice
    B. It is easier to decipher tone and purpose through Twitter or Facebook than through personal communication
    C. Most of the people who would be interested in your brand or service are comfortable and familiar with using social media
    D. Almost anyone can step into a media relations role if primarily using social media, because it is easy to communicate effectively through social media platforms

    2.____

3. You are tasked with building publicity for the upcoming reveal of a new art installation in the town you work in. Your boss tells you to contact journalists, reporters and bloggers to help spread the word. Which of the following would be the MOST effective way of getting the media to help build coverage?
    A. Send out a mass e-mail to any media members in the area detailing the art installation and why you need coverage for it
    B. Call each media outlet and find out who would most likely cover and build publicity for your project. Then reach out to them either face-to-face or through a phone call
    C. Using Twitter, tweet at the media members and introduce yourself and your art installation and ask them to help spread the word
    D. None of the above

    3.____

4. When using written communication, which of the following is a MAJOR challenge of writing to listeners?
    A. Providing lots of statistics
    B. Grabbing the attention of the listener quickly
    C. Providing information that is easily reviewed
    D. Presenting lots of incidentals

    4.____

5. In order to communicate well in writing, which of the following pieces of advice sounds good but doesn't actually help you?
   A. Write material for all audiences rather than focusing on one
   B. Think before writing
   C. Write simply and with clarity
   D. Write and rewrite until you have a polished, finished product

6. You send out a public newsletter that details a project that your team is currently working on. One week later, an employee on your team tells you she has received multiple phone calls from confused constituents claiming that the newsletter's readability was low. When you send out a corrected newsletter, you need to make sure that your communication is easy to
   A. read   B. hear   C. edit   D. comprehend

7. You work for a biomedical company as a public outreach advocate. One day, an exciting e-mail circulates internally that states one of your scientists has discovered a cure for leukemia and your supervisor tasks you with writing the release. When writing the release, the newsworthy element inherent in the story is
   A. oddity   B. conflict   C. impact   D. proximity

8. When communicating with the public through the Internet, news releases
   A. should not be sent via e-mail
   B. should be succinct
   C. should be sent via "snail mail"
   D. none of the above

9. What is the MAJOR advantage of organizational publications? Their ability to
   A. give sponsoring organizations a means of uncontrolled communications
   B. deliver specific, detailed information to narrowly defined target publics
   C. avoid the problems typically associated with two-way media
   D. provide a revenue source for sponsoring organizations

10. You are confronted by a question from a reporter that you do not know the answer to. What should you do?
    A. Give them other information you are certain is right
    B. Tell them that information is "off the record" and will be distributed later
    C. Say "no comment" rather than look like you're uninformed
    D. Admit that you don't know but promise to provide the information later

11. Often times, an organization will run situation analysis before they share information with the public. Which one of these "internal factors" is usually associated with a situational analysis?
    A. A communication audit
    B. Community focus groups
    C. A list of media contacts
    D. Strategy suggestions

12. When you are hired, your first task is to start a process of identifying who are involved and affected by a situation central to your organization. This process is MOST commonly referred to as a(n)
    A. situation interview
    B. communication audit
    C. exploratory survey
    D. stakeholder analysis

12.____

13. Once a public outreach plan is in the summative evaluation phase, which of the following is generally associated with it?
    A. Impact
    B. Implementation
    C. Attitude change
    D. Preparation

13.____

14. Which of the following Internet-related challenges is MOST significant in the public relations field?
    A. Finding stable, cost-effective internet provides
    B. Representing clients using new social media environments
    C. Staying abreast of changing technology
    D. Training staff to use social media

14.____

15. Which of the following BEST defines a public issue? Any
    A. problem that brings a public lawsuit
    B. concern that is of mutual distress to competitors
    C. issue that is of mutual concern to an organization and its stakeholders
    D. problem that is not a concern to an organization and/or one of its stakeholders

15.____

16. A handful of people are posting misleading and/or negative information about your organization. What is the MOST proactive approach to handling this situation?
    A. Buy up enough shares in the site where the negative posts are, and prevent those users from posting again
    B. Post anonymous comments on the sites to help combat the negativity
    C. Prepare news releases that discredit the inaccuracies
    D. Make policy changes to address complaints highlighted on the sites

16.____

17. Your supervisor has recently asked you to review present and future realities for interacting with the public. Why is it important to continually review these?
    A. It helps develop your vision statement
    B. It helps interpret trends for management
    C. It helps construe the organization's business plan
    D. To know what path the company should pursue

17.____

18. You are the community relations director for the public water utility plant that has been the focus of a group of activists who are opposed to the addition of fluoride to drinking water. These objectors are not only at the plant each day, but they are also very active on social media inciting negativity towards the practice. As the director of the plant, you have overwhelming evidence that contradicts what the protestors are arguing. You want to combat their social media with your own internet plan. Which of the following is the MOST appropriate action for you to take?
    A. Use utility employees to write the blog, posing as healthcare professionals
    B. Reach out to medical professionals to volunteer to tweet and message community members under their own identities, but with no reference to the utility company
    C. Write a blog yourself, identifying yourself as an employee, and quote the scientific opinions of a variety of sources
    D. Pay for medical professionals to respond through the internet, identifying the utility as their sponsor, but without disclosing the compensation

18.____

19. You have recently completed an advertising campaign to help assuage the anger of the community at changes in the upcoming summer program for the city. Which of the following measurements would be MOST effective for evaluating the campaign's impact on audience attitude?
    A. A content analysis of media coverage
    B. Studying blog postings about the issue
    C. Analyzing pre- and post-numbers of people signed up for the summer programs
    D. Conducting a pre- and post-analysis of public opinions

19.____

20. In order to measure how policy changes will affect the public, you recommend that your supervisors first run a focus group for research. They like the idea, but want you to be in charge of running the group. Which of the following should you keep in mind as you form the focus group?
    A. Participants need to be randomly selected
    B. Make sure participants are radically different from one another so you get a range of opinions
    C. Include at least seven or more people in the group. Otherwise, the sample is too small to draw any conclusions.
    D. Formulate a research plan and use it as a script so you can make sure the results are ones that will work for you and your supervisors

20.____

21. The public university has recently come under fire for not offering enough tuition savings options for students. You have been hired to help promote the programs they offer including new savings programs. What is the MOST appropriate first step for you to take?
    A. Research pricing and development costs for the services
    B. Develop a survey to discover which factors impact families' savings
    C. Conduct a situation analysis to gain better understanding of the issues
    D. Hold a focus group to determine which messages would be most effective for your program

21.____

5 (#2)

22. After receiving feedback from the public on a new program, you are concerned the results have been tainted by courtesy bias. You plan on sending out a new questionnaire, but you need to make sure the bias is discouraged in it. Which of the following techniques will be MOST effective at decreasing the partiality?
    A. Make questionnaire responses confidential
    B. Employ an outside firm to run the survey
    C. Offer a larger range of responses in the survey
    D. Both "A" and "C"

22.____

23. You have just relocated from Omaha, Nebraska to a branch in Chicago, Illinois. In order to communicate well while in Chicago, you must remember that
    A. most publics have the same needs
    B. all publics are most interested only in technology you are using
    C. each audience has its own special needs and require different types of communication
    D. all audiences' needs overlap

23.____

24. Recently, the Parks and Recreation Department has come under fire because it has been accused of too much marketing and not enough public relations. Which of the following, if true, would lend credibility to these accusations?
    A. Employees are focused on signing citizens up for as many different camps and activities available over the summer as possible
    B. Management consistently tries to send appreciation gifts to members of the community when they have volunteered or attending an activity sponsored by the Park district
    C. Weekly meetings are held to determine how to best improve the Park district's image as it relates to consumers
    D. Parks and Recreation is primarily focused on making sure the public enjoys their activities and trusts them to put on educational programs for the children

24.____

25. During your speech, a community member stands up and accuses you of "spinning" a story. Which of the following BEST describes their accusation?
    A. You are relating a message through an agreed-upon ethical practice within the public relations community
    B. You are twisting a message to create performance where there is none
    C. You are trying to preserve hard-earned credibility
    D. You are providing the media with balanced and accurate information

25.____

KEY (CORRECT ANSWERS)

1. D
2. A
3. C
4. B
5. D

6. D
7. C
8. B
9. B
10. D

11. A
12. D
13. A
14. C
15. C

16. B
17. A
18. C
19. D
20. A

21. C
22. D
23. C
24. A
25. B

TEST 3

DIRECTIONS: Each question or incomplete statement is followed by several suggested answers or completions. Select the one that BEST answers the question or completes the statement. *PRINT THE LETTER OF THE CORRECT ANSWER IN THE SPACE AT THE RIGHT.*

1. In order to be successful in relating to the public, all of the following are vital EXCEPT
    A. performance
    B. relationship building
    C. formal education
    D. diversity of experience

    1.____

2. Which of the following is TRUE of communicating well regarding public relations experts?
    A. It will differentiate you and your role from others with special skills in the organization you work for
    B. It should be handled delicately in order to avoid upsetting stakeholders
    C. It is not as important as looking fashionable
    D. It is less important than understanding bureaucratic peculiarities

    2.____

3. You are critiquing a staffer who will lead an important meeting in two days and you note that she keeps using words that are steeped with connotation. You tell her to be careful of these words. Why?
    A. They transmit meaning too clearly, and you always want to leave wiggle room in your meaning
    B. They transmit the dictionary definition of a word that makes for a boring presentation
    C. They transmit meaning with an emotional overtone that could lead to misunderstanding in an overall message
    D. They lend themselves to stereotyping

    3.____

4. If you are trying to avoid biasing your intended audience, which of the following factors could help with that?
    A. Symbols
    B. Objective reporting by media
    C. Semantics
    D. Peers

    4.____

5. Of the following, which trait is MOST desirable when working with the public?
    A. Having the "gift for gab"
    B. Being an elite strategist
    C. Being able to leap organizational boundaries
    D. Performing well, especially in crises

    5.____

6. Which of the following areas is likely to see continual growth in the practice of public relations?
    A. Healthcare
    B. Social media
    C. Law enforcement
    D. None of the above

    6.____

7. What is the MOST commonly used public relations tactic?
   A. A news release
   B. A special event
   C. A PSA (public service announcement)
   D. A full feature news article

8. You have just been assigned to help with a new advertising campaign that will promote the new services offered by your organization. One major component of the new campaign will focus on publicity through photographs. Knowing you need to get this part of the project right, which of the following is the BEST tip to remember when taking PR photos?
   A. Don't use action shots because they usually wind up blurry
   B. Make sure there is good contrast and sharp detail
   C. Ensure that the product/services are the biggest thing(s) in the photo
   D. Photograph multiple people rather than only one

9. Which of the following situations would merit holding a press conference?
   A. When a corporation is restructured
   B. When a new public relations employee has been hired
   C. When information is of minor relevance to a specific audience
   D. When there is a new product to be released

10. On average, how long should an announcement to the public last on the radio?
    A. 2 minutes   B. 20 seconds   C. 1 minute   D. 10 seconds

11. In educating the public, you need to develop a PR plan and analyze each situation that could arise. Which of the following should NOT be a part of the analysis?
    A. Research
    B. Message crafting
    C. Creating a problem statement
    D. Asking the 5 W's and the H

12. You are in charge of promoting an event in the near future, but social media is unavailable to you at this time. Which of the following is the BEST way to get your message out to the media and, therefore, the public?
    A. An Op-Ed piece in the local newspaper
    B. A press conference
    C. A newsletter
    D. A news release

13. In the past few months, you and your colleagues have been accused of "doublespeak". Which of the following excerpts from presentations you have used could you defend and explain why it would NOT be an example of "doublespeak"?
    A. You called combat "fighting"
    B. Fred referred to genocide as "ethnic cleansing"
    C. Your boss referred to recent layoffs as "downsizing"
    D. Susie called the janitor a "custodial engineer"

14. In relating to the public, which of the following reflects key words in defining modern day PR?   14._____
    A. Deliberate, public interest, management function
    B. Persuasive, manipulative, improvisation
    C. Management, technical, flexible
    D. Influential, creative, evaluative

15. How is educating and relating to the public different from being a journalist, marketing agent, or advertiser?   15._____
    A. It is more focused on advocacy
    B. It is about getting "free" press coverage
    C. It is about building relationships with various demographics
    D. All of the above

16. Of the following, what is the BEST tactic for learning employee attitudes?   16._____
    A. Internal communications audit   B. Research
    C. Conference meeting   D. Both A and B

17. When releasing news to the public, you should make sure it reads at a _____-grade reading level.   17._____
    A. 5th   B. 12th   C. 9th   D. 7th

18. If you are using a euphemism that actually changes the meaning/impact of a concept you are trying to relay, what is that called?   18._____
    A. Insider language   B. Doublespeak
    C. Stylizing   D. Plagiarism

19. Which of the following should be included in a public relations campaign if you want to ensure people will hear, understand, and believe your message?   19._____
    A. Repetition   B. Imagery
    C. Thoroughness   D. Acceptance

20. In PR, what is it called when you track coverage and compare it over a period of time?   20._____
    A. Bookmarking   B. Benchmarking
    C. Comparison analysis D. Correspondence

21. What is a baseline study PRIMARILY used for?   21._____
    A. To determine changes in audience perception and attitude
    B. To figure out how well your company is doing in the marketplace compared to your competitors
    C. To find out the cost of buying space taken up by a particular article if that article is an advertisement
    D. None of the above

22. Of the following people, who would BEST be considered a modern role model for successful public relations?
    A. Phineas T. Barnum (Barnum and Bailey)
    B. Ivy Lee
    C. Andrew Jackson
    D. Sir Walter Raleigh

23. If your organization has recently participated in a "publicity stunt," what type of PR strategy have you just used?
    A. Community
    B. Lobbying
    C. News management
    D. Crisis management

24. You tell your supervisor that you want to start using video press releases. When he presses you to explain why, you tell him that you want to take advantage of the fact that
    A. many news agencies don't review them ahead of broadcasting
    B. most reporters hired to create them have contacts within the industry
    C. they cover stories that some local news organizations cannot
    D. the production value may be better than those at local stations

25. A _____ is a type of news leak in which the source reveals large policy changes are on the table.
    A. disclosure   B. hook   C. exclusive   D. trial balloon

KEY (CORRECT ANSWERS)

1. C
2. B
3. C
4. B
5. D

6. B
7. A
8. B
9. D
10. C

11. B
12. D
13. A
14. A
15. D

16. D
17. C
18. B
19. A
20. B

21. A
22. B
23. C
24. C
25. D

TEST 4

DIRECTIONS: Each question or incomplete statement is followed by several suggested answers or completions. Select the one that BEST answers the question or completes the statement. *PRINT THE LETTER OF THE CORRECT ANSWER IN THE SPACE AT THE RIGHT.*

1. The Facial Feedback Hypothesis is a popular nonverbal theory that is BEST defined as
    A. people mirroring each other's facial expressions
    B. emotions leading to certain facial expressions
    C. facial expression can lead to the experience of certain emotions
    D. looking into a mirror while making a facial expression can cause one to change their facial expression

1.____

2. Of the following, which is NOT recognized as a function of smiling?
    A. It provides feedback.
    B. It signals disinterest.
    C. It helps establish rapport.
    D. It signals attentiveness.

2.____

3. When facial expressions are limited by cultural expectations, that is referred to as
    A. display rules
    B. syntactic displays
    C. adaptors
    D. interaction intensification

3.____

4. Of the following, which is recognized as part of the six basic emotions across cultures globally?
    A. Guilt
    B. Happiness
    C. Fear
    D. Both B and C

4.____

5. Which kinds of communication scenarios are more likely to see leadership roles develop from?
    A. Small group
    B. Intrapersonal communication
    C. Face-to-face public communication
    D. Text messaging

5.____

6. Which of the following highlights the key difference between small group communication and organizational communication?
    A. Feedback is easier and more immediate in organizational.
    B. Communication is more informal in small group communication.
    C. The message is easier to adapt to the specific needs of the receiver in organizational communication.
    D. People are more spread out in small group communication.

6.____

7. Which of the following would be an example of mediated communication?
    A. A principal addresses the student body in a speech.
    B. Two friends communicate while they work together in class.
    C. An employee texts his coworkers to see if they want to hang out after work.
    D. Three friends joke with one another while attending a concert.

7.____

8. Which of the following is FALSE concerning the way interpersonal relationships can affect us physically?
   A. Without interpersonal relationships, we can become sick
   B. These interpersonal relationships are necessary for humans; according to most research, humans raised in isolation are less healthy than those raised with others
   C. Humans are not the only mammals that need relationships in order to survive and thrive
   D. Interpersonal relationships are necessary until about age 12, but not later in adulthood

9. Which of the following is a characteristic of public relationships as they compare to private relationships?
   A. Intrinsic rewards
   B. Normative rules
   C. Use of particularistic knowledge
   D. Small number of intimates

10. When someone asks how you know they were angry, it is likely they fall into which style of facial expressions?
    A. Withholder
    B. Revealer
    C. Frozen-affect expressor
    D. Unwitting expressor

11. The theory of expectancy violations is BEST defined as
    A. nonverbal behavior reciprocated based primarily on positive or negative valence and the perceived reward value of the other person
    B. the process of intimacy exchange within a dyad relationship
    C. a social rule that says we should repay in kind what another has provided us
    D. none of the above

12. If an employee has a very good idea of what is and is not socially acceptable in any given situation, which kind of linguistic competence is she strong in?
    A. Phonemic   B. Syntactic   C. Pragmatic   D. Semantic

13. Which of the following would NOT be considered sexist language?
    A. Although a girl, Sonia is very brave.
    B. A gorgeous model, Johnny also likes to use his surfboard on the weekends.
    C. Jimmy's brother is a male nurse.
    D. None; all are considered to be sexist.

14. What is it called when individual experience, and NOT conventional agreement, creates meaning?
    A. Small talk communication
    B. Denotative meaning
    C. Connotative meaning
    D. Self-reflexive communication

15. Which of the following kinds of communication do students spend the MOST time engaged in?
    A. Listening   B. Writing   C. Reading   D. Speaking

16. Which of the following would be evidence of active listening? 16.____
    A. Maintain eye contact
    B. Nodding and making eye contact
    C. Asking for clarification
    D. All of the above

17. When listening in an evaluative context, which of the following must be done 17.____
    for it to be considered successful?
    A. Precisely disseminate stimuli in a message
    B. Comprehend the intended meaning of a message
    C. Make critical assessments of the accuracy of the facts in a message
    D. All of the above

18. A friend visits one day and tells you she thinks her husband is cheating on her 18.____
    with his ex-wife. She tells you she doesn't know what to do because she can't
    imagine living without him. If you wanted to paraphrase, which of the following
    BEST exemplifies that?
    A. "You are feeling insecure because you don't have a very good
       relationship with your husband."
    B. "You're afraid your husband is seeing his ex-wife behind your back; you
       don't know what to do; and you can't live without him."
    C. "You're afraid that your husband may still have feelings for his ex-wife and
       you're afraid you'll lose him."
    D. "Don't worry; his ex-wife is not back with him. You're just being paranoid."

19. When we form impressions of others, when might the recency effect impact 19.____
    our assessments? If we
    A. focus on our own feelings instead of the feelings of others
    B. are motivated to be more accurate or expect to be held accountable for
       our own perceptions
    C. engage in self-monitoring of our behaviors
    D. employ the discounting rule

20. Which of the following BEST defines a "modal self"? 20.____
    A. The ideal person for a social order
    B. A person who does not go to extremes
    C. The kind of self valued in the 20th century but not the 21st century
    D. The person who monitors his own behavior in social situations

21. Which of the following is TRUE of today's society? 21.____
    A. People are less selfish than they have ever been.
    B. People spend most of their time trying to be a single, unitary self.
    C. People have many short-lived relationships leading to their notions of
       themselves changing easily.
    D. People try to be frugal, honorable, and self-sacrificing.

22. A man's childhood consisted of a dismissing attachment style. Which of the following behaviors will he MOST likely exhibit as an adult?
    A. Anxiousness and ambivalence
    B. Obsessive friendliness and dependence
    C. Autonomy and distance from others
    D. Rhetorical sensitivity

22.____

23. When practicing self-disclosure, which of the following is a good rule of thumb?
    A. Be sure to disclose more than your partner
    B. Reserve your most important disclosures for people you know well
    C. Ignore the style of disclosure; the only thing that is important is content
    D. All of the above

23.____

24. During your first meeting as project leader, you approach your group and inform them that John will serve as your assistant project leader. He will be responsible for chairing team meetings and establishing the agenda. When John is given this formal leadership position, what type of power does he have over the other members of the project?
    A. Legitimate   B. Reward   C. Expert   D. Punishment

24.____

25. If you bring an employee to lead a project because she is knowledgeable and skilled in the area the project focuses on, what type of power does she possess?
    A. Legitimate   B. Reward   C. Referent   D. Expert

25.____

KEY (CORRECT ANSWERS)

1.	C	11.	A
2.	B	12.	C
3.	A	13.	D
4.	D	14.	C
5.	A	15.	A
6.	B	16.	D
7.	C	17.	C
8.	D	18.	B
9.	B	19.	D
10.	D	20.	A

21. C
22. C
23. B
24. A
25. D

COMMUNICATION

EXAMINATION SECTION
TEST 1

DIRECTIONS: Each question or incomplete statement is followed by several suggested answers or completions. Select the one that BEST answers the question or completes the statement. *PRINT THE LETTER OF THE CORRECT ANSWER IN THE SPACE AT THE RIGHT.*

1. In some agencies the counsel to the agency head is given the right to bypass the chain of command and issue orders directly to the staff concerning matters that involve certain specific processes and practices.
   This situation MOST nearly illustrates the principle of _____ authority.
   A. the acceptance theory of
   B. multiple-linear
   C. splintered
   D. functional

2. It is commonly understood that communication is an important part of the administrative process.
   Which of the following is NOT a valid principle of the communication process in administration?
   A. The channels of communication should be spontaneous.
   B. The lines of communication should be as direct and as short as possible.
   C. Communications should be authenticated.
   D. The persons serving in communications centers should be competent.

3. Of the following, the one factor which is generally considered LEAST essential to successful committee operations is
   A. stating a clear definition of the authority and scope of the committee
   B. selecting the committee chairman carefully
   C. limiting the size of the committee to four persons
   D. limiting the subject matter to that which can be handled in group discussion

4. Of the following, the failure by line managers to accept and appreciate the benefits and limitations of a new program or system VERY FREQUENTLY can be traced to the
   A. budgetary problems involved
   B. resultant need to reduce staff
   C. lack of controls it engenders
   D. failure of top management to support its implementation

5. If a manager were thinking about using a committee of subordinates to solve an operating problem, which of the following would generally NOT be an advantage of such use of the committee approach?
   A. Improved coordination
   B. Low cost
   C. Increased motivation
   D. Integrated judgment

6. Every supervisor has many occasions to lead a conference or participate in a conference of some sort.
Of the following statements that pertain to conferences and conference leadership, which is generally considered to be MOST valid?
   A. Since World War II, the trend has been toward fewer shared decisions and more conferences.
   B. The most important part of a conference leader's job is to direct discussion.
   C. In providing opportunities for group interaction, management should avoid consideration of its past management philosophy.
   D. A good administrator cannot lead a good conference if he is a poor public speaker.

7. Of the following, it is usually LEAST desirable for a conference leader to
   A. call the name of a person after asking a question
   B. summarize proceedings periodically
   C. make a practice of repeating questions
   D. ask a question without indicating who is to reply

8. Assume that, in a certain organization, a situation has developed in which there is little difference in status or authority between individuals.
Which of the following would be the MOST likely result with regard to communication in this organization?
   A. Both the accuracy and flow of communication will be improved.
   B. Both the accuracy and flow of communication will substantially decrease.
   C. Employees will seek more formal lines of communication.
   D. Neither the flow nor the accuracy of communication will be improved over the former hierarchical structure.

9. The main function of many agency administrative officers is "information management." Information that is received by an administrative officer may be classified as active or passive, depending upon whether or not it requires the recipient to take some action.
Of the following, the item received which is clearly the MOST active information is
   A. an appointment of a new staff member
   B. a payment voucher for a new desk
   C. a press release concerning a past event
   D. the minutes of a staff meeting

10. Of the following, the one LEAST considered to be a communication barrier is
    A. group feedback   B. charged words
    C. selective perception D. symbolic meanings

11. Management studies support the hypothesis that, in spite of the tendency of employees to censor the information communicated to their supervisor, subordinates are more likely to communicate problem-oriented information UPWARD when they have a
    A. long period of service in the organization
    B. high degree of trust in the supervisor
    C. high educational level
    D. low status on the organizational ladder

11.____

12. Electronic data processing equipment can produce more information faster than can be generated by any other means.
In view of this, the MOST important problem faced by management at present is to
    A. keep computers fully occupied
    B. find enough computer personnel
    C. assimilate and properly evaluate the information
    D. obtain funds to establish appropriate information systems

12.____

13. A well-designed management information system essentially provides each executive and manager the information he needs for
    A. determining computer time requirements
    B. planning and measuring results
    C. drawing a new organization chart
    D. developing a new office layout

13.____

14. It is generally agreed that management policies should be periodically reappraised and restated in accordance with current conditions.
Of the following, the approach which would be MOST effective in determining whether a policy should be revised is to
    A. conduct interviews with staff members at all levels in order to ascertain the relationship between the policy and actual practice
    B. make proposed revisions in the policy and apply it to current problems
    C. make up hypothetical situations using both the old policy and a revised version in order to make comparisons
    D. call a meeting of top level staff in order to discuss ways of revising the policy

14.____

15. Your superior has asked you to notify division employees of an important change in one of the operating procedures described in the division manual. Every employee presently has a copy of this manual.
Which of the following is normally the MOST practical way to get the employees to understand such a change?
    A. Notify each employee individually of the change and answer any questions he might have
    B. Send a written notice to key personnel, directing them to inform the people under them

15.____

C. Call a general meeting, distribute a corrected page for the manual, and discuss the change
D. Send a memo to employees describing the change in general terms and asking them to make the necessary corrections in their copies of the manual

16. Assume that the work in your department involves the use of any technical terms.
In such a situation, when you are answering inquiries from the general public, it would usually be BEST to
    A. use simple language and avoid the technical terms
    B. employ the technical terms whenever possible
    C. bandy technical terms freely, but explain each term in parentheses
    D. apologize if you are forced to use a technical term

16.____

17. Suppose that you receive a telephone call from someone identifying himself as an employee in another city department who asks to be given information which your own department regards as confidential.
Which of the following is the BEST way of handling such a request?
    A. Give the information requested, since your caller as official standing
    B. Grant the request, provided the caller gives you a signed receipt
    C. Refuse the request, because you have no way of knowing whether the caller is really who he claims to be
    D. Explain that the information is confidential and inform the caller of the channels he must go through to have the information released to him

17.____

18. Studies show that office employees place high importance on the social and human aspects of the organization. What office employees like best about their jobs is the kind of people with whom they work. So strive hard to group people who are most likely to get along well together.
Based on this information, it is MOST reasonable to assume that office workers are most pleased to work in a group which
    A. is congenial   B. has high productivity
    C. allows individual creativity   D. is unlike other groups

18.____

19. A certain supervisor does not compliment members of his staff when they come up with good ideas. He feels that coming up with good ideas is part of the job and does not merit special attention.
This supervisor's practice is
    A. *poor*, because recognition for good ideas is a good motivator
    B. *poor*, because the staff will suspect that the supervisor has no good ideas of his own
    C. *good*, because it is reasonable to assume that employees will tell their supervisor of ways to improve office practice
    D. *good*, because the other members of the staff are not made to seem inferior by comparison

19.____

20. Some employees of a department have sent an anonymous letter containing many complaints to the department head.
Of the following, what is this MOST likely to show about the department?
    A. It is probably a good place to work.
    B. Communications are probably poor.
    C. The complaints are probably unjustified.
    D. These employees are probably untrustworthy.

20.____

21. Which of the following actions would usually be MOST appropriate for a supervisor to take after receiving an instruction sheet from his superior explaining a new procedure which is to be followed?
    A. Put the instruction sheet aside temporarily until he determines what is wrong with the old procedure.
    B. Call his superior and ask whether the procedure is one he must implement immediately.
    C. Write a memorandum to the superior asking for more details.
    D. Try the new procedure and advise the superior of any problems or possible improvements.

21.____

22. Of the following, which one is considered the PRIMARY advantage of using a committee to resolved a problem in an organization?
    A. No one person will be held accountable for the decision since a group of people was involved.
    B. People with different backgrounds give attention to the problem.
    C. The decision will take considerable time so there is unlikely to be a decision that will later be regretted.
    D. One person cannot dominate the decision-making process.

22.____

23. Employees in a certain office come to their supervisor with all their complaints about the office and the work. Almost every employee has had at least one minor complaint at some time.
The situation with respect to complaints in this office may BEST be described as probably
    A. *good*; employees who complain care about their jobs and work hard
    B. *good*; grievances brought out into the open can be corrected
    C. *bad*; only serious complaints should be discussed
    D. *bad*; it indicates the staff does not have confidence in the administration

23.____

24. The administrator who allows his staff to suggest ways to do their work will usually find that
    A. this practice contributes to high productivity
    B. the administrator's ideas produce greater output
    C. clerical employees suggest inefficient work methods
    D. subordinate employees resent performing a management function

24.____

25. The MAIN purpose for a supervisor's questioning the employees at a conference he is holding is to
    A. stress those areas of information covered but not understood by the participants
    B. encourage participants to think through the problem under discussion
    C. catch those subordinates who are not paying attention
    D. permit the more knowledgeable participants to display their grasp of the problems being discussed

25.____

KEY (CORRECT ANSWERS)

1.	D		11.	B
2.	A		12.	C
3.	C		13.	B
4.	D		14.	A
5.	B		15.	C
6.	B		16.	A
7.	C		17.	D
8.	D		18.	A
9.	A		19.	A
10.	A		20.	B

21. D
22. B
23. B
24. A
25. B

TEST 2

DIRECTIONS: Each question or incomplete statement is followed by several suggested answers or completions. Select the one that BEST answers the question or completes the statement. *PRINT THE LETTER OF THE CORRECT ANSWER IN THE SPACE AT THE RIGHT.*

1. For a superior to use *consultative supervision* with his subordinates effectively, it is ESSENTIAL that he
   A. accept the fact that his formal authority will be weakened by the procedure
   B. admit that he does not know more than all his men together and that his ideas are not always best
   C. utilize a committee system so that the procedure is orderly
   D. make sure that all subordinates are consulted so that no one feels left out

   1.____

2. The *grapevine* is an informal means of communication in an organization. The attitude of a supervisor with respect to the grapevine should be to
   A. ignore it since it deals mainly with rumors and sensational information
   B. regard it as a serious danger which should be eliminated
   C. accept it as a real line of communication which should be listened to
   D. utilize it for most purposes instead of the official line of communication

   2.____

3. The supervisor of an office that must deal with the public should realize that planning in this type of work situation
   A. is useless because he does not know how many people will request service or what service they will request
   B. must be done at a higher level but that he should be ready to implement the results of such planning
   C. is useful primarily for those activities that are not concerned with public contact
   D. is useful for all the activities of the office, including those that relate to public contact

   3.____

4. Assume that it is your job to receive incoming telephone calls. Those calls which you cannot handle yourself have to be transferred to the appropriate office.
   If you receive an outside call for an extension line which is busy, the one of the following which you should do FIRST is to
   A. interrupt the person speaking on the extension and tell him a call is waiting
   B. tell the caller the line is busy and let him know every thirty seconds whether or not it is free
   C. leave the caller on "hold" until the extension is free
   D. tell the caller the line is busy and ask him if he wishes to wait

   4.____

5. Your superior has subscribed to several publications directly related to your division's work, and he has asked you to see to it that the publications are circulated among the supervisory personnel in the division. There are eight supervisors involved.
The BEST method of insuring that all eight see these publications is to
   A. place the publication in the division's general reference library as soon as it arrives
   B. inform each supervisor whenever a publication arrives and remind all of them that they are responsible for reading it
   C. prepare a standard slip that can be stapled to each publication, listing the eight supervisors and saying, "Please read, initial your name, and pass along"
   D. send a memo to the eight supervisors saying that they may wish to purchase individual subscriptions in their own names if they are interested in seeing each issue

6. Your superior has telephoned a number of key officials in your agency to ask whether they can meet at a certain time next month. He has found that they can all make it, and he has asked you to confirm the meeting.
Which of the following is the BEST way to confirm such a meeting?
   A. Note the meeting on your superior's calendar.
   B. Post a notice of the meeting on the agency bulletin board.
   C. Call the officials on the day of the meeting to remind them of the meeting.
   D. Write a memo to each official involved, repeating the time and place of the meeting.

7. Assume that a new city regulation requires that certain kinds of private organizations file information forms with your department. You have been asked to write the short explanatory message that will be printed on the front cover of the pamphlet containing the forms and instructions.
Which of the following would be the MOST appropriate way of beginning this message?
   A. Get the readers' attention by emphasizing immediately that there are legal penalties for organizations that fail to file before a certain date.
   B. Briefly state the nature of the enclosed forms and the types of organizations that must file.
   C. Say that your department is very sorry to have to put organizations to such an inconvenience.
   D. Quote the entire regulation adopted by the city, even if it is quite long and is expressed din complicated legal language.

8. Suppose that you have been told to make up the vacation schedule for the 18 employees in a particular unit. In order for the unit to operate effectively, only a few employees can be on vacation at the same time.
Which of the following is the MOST advisable approach in making up the schedule?
   A. Draw up a schedule assigning vacations in alphabetical order
   B. Find out when the supervisors want to take their vacations, and randomly assign whatever periods are left to the non-supervisory personnel

C. Assign the most desirable times to employees of longest standing and the least desirable times to the newest employees
D. Have all employees state their own preference, and then work out any conflicts in consultation with the people involved

9. Assume that you have been asked to prepare job descriptions for various positions in your department.
Which of the following are the basic points that should be covered in a *job description*?
   A. General duties and responsibilities of the position, with examples of day-to-day tasks
   B. Comments on the performances of present employees
   C. Estimates of the number of openings that may be available in each category during the coming year
   D. Instructions for carrying out the specific tasks assigned to your department

9._____

10. Of the following, the biggest DISADVANTAGE in allowing a free flow of communications in an agency is that such a free flow
    A. decreases creativity
    B. increases the use of the *grapevine*
    C. lengthens the chain of command
    D. reduces the executive's power to direct the flow of information

10._____

11. A downward flow of authority in an organization is one example of _____ communication.
    A. horizontal   B. informal   C. circular   D. vertical

11._____

12. Of the following, the one that would MOST likely block effective communication is
    A. concentration only on the issues at hand
    B. lack of interest or commitment
    C. use of written reports
    D. use of charts and graphs

12._____

13. An ADVANTAGE of the *lecture* as a teaching tool is that it
    A. enables a person to present his ideas to a large number of people
    B. allows the audience to retain a maximum of the information given
    C. holds the attention of the audience for the longest time
    D. enables the audience member to easily recall the main points

13._____

14. An ADVANTAGE of the *small-group* discussion as a teaching tool is that
    A. it always focuses attention on one person as the leader
    B. it places collective responsibility on the group as a whole
    C. its members gain experience by summarizing the ideas of others
    D. each member of the group acts as a member of a team

14._____

15. The one of the following that is an ADVANTAGE of a *large-group* discussion, when compared to a small-group discussion, is that the large-group discussion
    A. moves along more quickly than a small-group discussion
    B. allows its participants to feel more at ease, and speak out more freely
    C. gives the whole group a chance to exchange ideas on a certain subject at the same occasion
    D. allows its members to feel a greater sense of personal responsibility

15.____

KEY (CORRECT ANSWERS)

1. D	6. D	11. D
2. C	7. B	12. B
3. D	8. D	13. A
4. D	9. A	14. D
5. C	10. D	15. C

PREPARING WRITTEN MATERIAL

PARAGRAPH REARRANGEMENT
COMMENTARY

The sentences that follow are in scrambled order. You are to rearrange them in proper order and indicate the letter choice containing the correct answer at the space at the right.

Each group of sentences in this section is actually a paragraph presented in scrambled order. Each sentence in the group has a place in that paragraph; no sentence is to be left out. You are to read each group of sentences and decide upon the best order in which to put the sentences so as to form a well-organized paragraph.

The questions in this section measure the ability to solve a problem when all the facts relevant to its solution are not given.

More specifically, certain positions of responsibility and authority require the employee to discover connection between events sometimes, apparently, unrelated. In order to do this, the employee will find it necessary to correctly infer that unspecified events have probably occurred or are likely to occur. This ability becomes especially important when action must be taken on incomplete information.

Accordingly, these questions require competitors to choose among several suggested alternatives, each of which presents a different sequential arrangement of the events. Competitors must choose the MOST logical of the suggested sequences.

In order to do so, they may be required to draw on general knowledge to infer missing concepts or events that are essential to sequencing the given events. Competitors should be careful to infer only what is essential to the sequence. The plausibility of the wrong alternatives will always require the inclusion of unlikely events or of additional chains of events which are NOT essential to sequencing the given events.

It's very important to remember that you are looking for the best of the four possible choices, and that the best choice of all may not even be one of the answers you're given to choose from.

There is no one right way to solve these problems. Many people have found it helpful to first write out the order of the sentences, as they would have arranged them, on their scrap paper before looking at the possible answers. If their optimum answer is there, this can save them some time. If it isn't, this method can still give insight into solving the problem. Others find it most helpful to just go through each of the possible choices, contrasting each as they go along. You should use whatever method feels comfortable and works for you.

While most of these types of questions are not that difficult, we've added a higher percentage of the difficult type, just to give you more practice. Usually there are only one or two questions on this section that contain such subtle distinctions that you're unable to answer confidently. And you then may find yourself stuck deciding between two possible choices, neither of which you're sure about.

EXAMINATION SECTION
TEST 1

DIRECTIONS: The following groups of sentences need to be arranged in an order that makes sense. Select the letter preceding the sequence that represents the BEST sentence order. *PRINT THE LETTER OF THE CORRECT ANSWER IN THE SPACE AT THE RIGHT.*

1.
   I. The keyboard was purposely designed to be a little awkward to slow typists down.
   II. The arrangement of letters on the keyboard of a typewriter was not designed for the convenience of the typist.
   III. Fortunately, no one is suggesting that a new keyboard be designed right away.
   IV. If one were, we would have to learn to type all over again.
   V. The reason was that the early machines were slower than the typists and would jam easily.

   The CORRECT answer is:
   A. I, III, IV, II, V B. II, V, I, IV, III
   C. V, I, II, III, IV D. II, I, V, III, IV

   1.____

2.
   I. The majority of the new service jobs are part-time or low-paying.
   II. According to the U.S. Bureau of Labor Statistics, jobs in the service sector constitute 72% of all jobs in this country.
   III. If more and more workers receive less and less money, who will buy the goods and services needed to keep the economy going?
   IV. The service sector is by far the fastest growing part of the United States economy.
   V. Some economists look upon this trend with great concern.

   The CORRECT answer is:
   A. II, IV, I, V, III B. II, III, IV, I, V
   C. V, IV, II, III, I D. III, I, II, IV, V

   2.____

3.
   I. They can also affect one's endurance.
   II. This can stabilize blood sugar levels, and ensure that the brain is receiving a steady, constant, supply of glucose, so that one is *hitting on all cylinders* while taking the test.
   III. By food, we mean real food, not junk food or unhealthy snacks.
   IV. For this reason, it is important not to skip a meal, and to bring food with you to the exam.
   V. One's blood sugar levels can affect how clearly one is able to think and concentrate during an exam.

   The CORRECT answer is:
   A. V, IV, II, III, I B. V, II, I, IV, III
   C. V, I, IV, III, II D. V, IV, I, III, II

   3.____

4. I. Those who are the embodiment of desire are absorbed in material quests, and those who are the embodiment of feeling are warriors who value power more than possession.
    II. These qualities are in everyone, but in different degrees.
    III. But those who value understanding yearn not for goods or victory, but for knowledge.
    IV. According to Plato, human behavior flows from three main sources: desire, emotion, and knowledge.
    V. In the perfect state, the industrial forces would produce but not rule, the military would protect but not rule, and the forces of knowledge, the philosopher kings, would reign.
    The CORRECT answer is:
    A. IV, V, I, II, III
    B. V, I, II, III, IV
    C. IV, III, II, I, V
    D. IV, II, I, III, V

4.____

5. I. Of the more than 26,000 tons of garbage produced daily in New York City, 12,000 tons arrive daily at Fresh Kills.
    II. In a month, enough garbage accumulates there to fill the Empire State Building.
    III. In 1937, the Supreme Court halted the practice of dumping the trash of New York City into the sea.
    IV. Although the garbage is compacted, in a few years the mounds of garbage at Fresh Kills will be the highest points south of Maine's Mount Desert Island on the Eastern Seaboard.
    V. Instead, tugboats now pull barges of much of the trash to Staten Island and the largest landfill in the world, Fresh Kills.
    The CORRECT answer is:
    A. III, V, IV, I, II
    B. III, V, II, IV, I
    C. III, V, I, II, IV
    D. III, II, V, IV, I

5.____

6. I. Communists rank equality very high, but freedom very low.
    II. Unlike communists, conservatives place a high value on freedom and a very low value on equality.
    III. A recent study demonstrated that one way to classify people's political beliefs is to look at the importance placed on two words: freedom and equality.
    IV. Thus, by demonstrating how members of these groups feel about the two words, the study has proved to be useful for political analysts in several European countries.
    V. According to the study, socialists and liberals rank both freedom and equality very high, while fascists rate both very low.
    The CORRECT answer is:
    A. III, V, I, II, IV
    B. V, IV, III, I, II
    C. III, V, IV, II, I
    D. III, I, II, IV, V

6.____

7.
I. "Can there be anything more amazing than this?"
II. If the riddle is successfully answered, his dead brothers will be brought back to life.
III. "Even though man sees those around him dying every day," says Dharmaraj, "he still believes and acts as if he were immortal."
IV. "What is the cause of ceaseless wonder?" asks the Lord of the Lake.
V. In the ancient epic, The Mahabharata, a riddle is asked of one of the Pandava brothers.
The CORRECT answer is:
A. V, II, I, IV, III
B. V, IV, III, I, II
C. V, II, IV, III, I
D. V, II, IV, I, III

7.____

8.
I. On the contrary, the two main theories—the cooperative (neoclassical) theory and the radical (labor theory)—clearly rest on very different assumptions, which have very different ethical overtones.
II. The distribution of income is the primary factor in determining the relative levels of material well-being that different groups or individuals attain.
III. Of all issues in economics, the distribution of income is one of the most controversial.
IV. The neoclassical theory tends to support the existing income distribution (or minor changes), while the labor theory ends to support substantial changes in the way income is distributed.
V. The intensity of the controversy reflects the fact that different economic theories are not purely neutral, *detached* theories with no ethical or moral implications.
The CORRECT answer is:
A. II, I, V, IV, III
B. III, II, V, I, IV
C. III, V, II, I, IV
D. III, V, IV, I, II

8.____

9.
I. The pool acts as a broker and ensures that the cheapest power gets used first.
II. Every six seconds, the pool's computer monitors all of the generating stations in the state and decides which to ask for more power and which to cut back.
III. The buying and selling of electrical power is handled by the New York Power Pool in Guilderland, New York.
IV. This is to the advantage of both the buying and selling utilities.
V. The pool began operation in 1970, and consists of the state's eight electric utilities.
The CORRECT answer is:
A. V, I, II, III, IV
B. IV, II, I, III, V
C. III, V, I, IV, II
D. V, III, IV, II, I

9.____

10. I. Modern English is much simpler grammatically than Old English.
    II. Finnish grammar is very complicated; there are some fifteen cases, for example.
    III. Chinese, a very old language, may seem to be the exception, but it is the great number of characters/words that must be mastered that makes it so difficult to learn, not its grammar.
    IV. The newest literary language—that is, written as well as spoken—is Finish, whose literary roots go back only to about the middle of the nineteenth century.
    V. Contrary to popular belief, the longer a language is been in use the simpler its grammar—not the reverse.

    The CORRECT answer is:
    A. IV, I, II, III, V
    B. V, I, IV, II, III
    C. I, II, IV, III, V
    D. IV, II, III, I, V

10.____

KEY (CORRECT ANSWERS)

1. D
2. A
3. C
4. D
5. C

6. A
7. C
8. B
9. C
10. B

# TEST 2

DIRECTIONS: This type of question tests your ability to recognize accurate paraphrasing, well-constructed paragraphs, and appropriate style and tone. It is important that the answer you select contains only the facts or concepts given in the original sentences. It is also important that you be aware of incomplete sentences, inappropriate transitions, unsupported opinions, incorrect usage, and illogical sentence order. Paragraphs that do not include all the necessary facts and concepts, that distort them, or that add new ones are not considered correct.

The format for this section may vary. Sometimes, long paragraphs are given, and emphasis is placed on style and organization. Our first five questions are of this type. Other times, the paragraphs are shorter, and there is less emphasis on style and more emphasis on accurate representation of information. Our second group of five questions are of this nature.

For each of Questions 1 through 10, select the paragraph that BEST expresses the ideas contained in the sentences above it. *PRINT THE LETTER OF THE CORRECT ANSWER IN THE SPACE AT THE RIGHT.*

1.
   I. Listening skills are very important for managers.
   II. Listening skills are not usually emphasized.
   III. Whenever managers are depicted in books, manuals or the media, they are always talking, never listening.
   IV. We'd like you to read the enclosed handout on listening skills and to try to consciously apply them this week.
   V. We guarantee they will improve the quality of your interactions.

   A. Unfortunately, listening skills are not usually emphasized for managers. Managers are always depicted as talking, never listening. We'd like you to read the enclosed handout on listening skills. Please try to apply these principles this week. If you do, we guarantee they will improve the quality of your interactions.
   B. The enclosed handout on listening skills will be important improving the quality of your interactions. We guarantee it. All you have to do is take sometime this week to read and to consciously try to apply the principles. Listening skills are very important for manages, but they are not usually emphasized. Whenever managers are depicted in books, manuals or the media, they are always talking, never listening.
   C. Listening well is one of the most important skills a manager can have, yet it's not usually given much attention. Think about any representation of managers in books, manuals, or in the media that you may have seen. They're always talking, never listening. We'd like you to read the enclosed handout on listening skills and consciously try to apply them the rest of the week. We guarantee you will see a difference in the quality of your interactions.

1.____

D. Effective listening, one very important tool in the effective manager's arsenal, is usually not emphasized enough. The usual depiction of managers in books, manuals or the media is one in which they are always talking, never listening. We'd like you to read the enclosed handout and consciously try to apply the information contained therein throughout the rest of the week. We feel sure that you will see a marked difference in the quality of your interactions.

2.
I. Chekhov wrote three dramatic masterpieces which share certain themes and formats: Uncle Vanya, The Cherry Orchard, and The Three Sisters.
II. They are primarily concerned with the passage of time and how this erodes human aspirations.
III. The plays are haunted by the ghosts of the wasted life.
IV. The characters are concerned with life's lesser problems; however, such as the inability to make decisions, loyalty to the wrong cause, and the inability to be clear.
V. This results in sweet, almost aching, type of a sadness referred to as Chekhovian.

2.____

A. Chekhov wrote three dramatic masterpieces: Uncle Vanya, The Cherry Orchard, and The Three Sisters. These masterpieces share certain themes and formats: the passage of time, how time erodes human aspirations, and the ghosts of wasted life. Each masterpiece is characterized by a sweet, almost aching, type of sadness that has become known as Chekhovian. The sweetness of this sadness hinges on the fact that it is not the great tragedies of life which are destroying these characters, but their minor flaws: indecisiveness, misplaced loyalty, unclarity.
B. The Cherry Orchard, Uncle Vanya, and The Three Sisters are three dramatic masterpieces written by Chekhov that use similar formats to explore a common theme. Each is primarily concerned with the way that passing time wears down human aspirations, and each is haunted by the ghosts of the wasted life. The characters are shown struggling futilely with the lesser problems of life: indecisiveness, loyalty to the wrong cause, and the inability to be clear. These struggles create a mood of sweet, almost aching, sadness that has become known as Chekhovian.
C. Chekhov's dramatic masterpieces are, along with The Cherry Orchard, Uncle Vanya, and The Three Sisters. These plays share certain thematic and formal similarities. They are concerned most of all with the passage of time and the way in which time erodes human aspirations. Each play is haunted by the specter of the wasted life. Chekhov's characters are caught, however, by life's lesser snares: indecisiveness, loyalty to the wrong cause, and unclarity. The characteristic mood is a sweet, almost aching type of sadness that has come to be known as Chekhovian.
D. A Chekhovian mood is characterized by sweet, almost aching, sadness. The term comes from three dramatic tragedies by Chekhov which revolve around the sadness of a wasted life. The three masterpieces (Uncle Vanya, The Three Sisters, and The Cherry Orchard) share the same

theme and format. The plays are concerned with how the passage of time erodes human aspirations. They are peopled with characters who are struggling with life's lesser problems. These are people who are indecisive, loyal to the wrong causes, or are unable to make themselves clear.

3.   I. Movie previews have often helped producers decide which parts of movies they should take out or leave in.
  II. The first 1933 preview of King Kong was very helpful to the producers because many people ran screaming from the theater and would not return when four men first attacked by Kong were eaten by giant spiders.
  III. The 1950 premiere of Sunset Boulevard resulted in the filming of an entirely new beginning, and a delay of six months in the film's release.
  IV. In the original opening scene, William Holden was in a morgue talking with thirty-six other "corpses" about the ways some of them had died.
  V. When he began to tell them of his life with Gloria Swanson, the audience found this hilarious, instead of taking the scene seriously.

3._____

  A. Movie previews have often helped producers decide what parts of movies they should leave in or take out. For example, the first preview of King Kong in 1933 was very helpful. In one scene, four men were first attacked by Kong and then eaten by giant spiders. Many members of the audience ran screaming from the theater and would not return. The premiere of the 1950 film Sunset Boulevard was also very helpful. In the original opening scene, William Holden was in a morgue with thirty-six other "corpses," discussing the ways some of them had died. When he began to tell them of his life with Gloria Swanson, the audience found this hilarious. They were supposed to take the scene seriously. The result was a delay of six months in the release of the film while a new beginning was added.
  B. Movie previews have often helped producers decide whether they should change various parts of a movie. After the 1933 preview of King Kong, a scene in which four men who had been attacked by Kong were eaten by giant spiders was taken out as many people ran screaming from the theater and would not return. The 1950 premiere of Sunset Boulevard also led to some changes. In the original opening scene, William Holden was in a morgue talking with thirty-six other "corpses" about the ways some of them had died. When he began to tell them of his life with Gloria Swanson, the audience found this hilarious, instead of taking the scene seriously.
  C. What do Sunset Boulevard and King Kong have in common? Both show the value of using movie previews to test audience reaction. The first 1933 preview of King Kong showed that a scene showing four men being eaten by giant spiders after having been attacked by Kong was too frightening for many people. They ran screaming from the theater and couldn't be coaxed back. The 1950 premiere of Sunset Boulevard was also a scream, but not the kind the producers intended. The movie opens

       with William Holden lying in a morgue discussing the ways they had died with thirty-six other "corpses." When he began to tell them of his life with Gloria Swanson, the audience couldn't take him seriously. Their laughter caused a six-month delay while the beginning was rewritten.
- D. Producers very often use movie previews to decide if changes are needed. The premiere of <u>Sunset Boulevard</u> in 1950 led to a new beginning and a six-month delay in film release. At the beginning, William Holden and thirty-six other "corpses" discuss the ways some of them died. Rather than taking this seriously, the audience thought it was hilarious when he began to tell them of his life with Gloria Swanson. The first 1933 preview of <u>King Kong</u> was very helpful for its producers because one scene so terrified the audience that many of them ran screaming from the theater and would not return. In this particular scene, four men who had first been attacked by Kong were eaten by giant spiders.

4.
- I. It is common for supervisors to view employees as "things" to be manipulated.
- II. This approach does not motivate employees, nor does the carrot-and-stick approach because employees often recognize these behaviors and resent them.
- III. Supervisors can change these behaviors by using self-inquiry and persistence.
- IV. The best managers genuinely respect those they work with, are supportive and helpful, and are interested in working as a team with those they supervise.
- V. They disagree with the Golden Rule that says "he or she who has the gold makes the rules."

4.____

    A. Some managers act as if they think the Golden Rule means "he or she who has the gold makes the rules." They show disrespect to employees by seeing them as "things" to be manipulated. Obviously, this approach does not motivate employees any more than the carrot-and-stick approach motivates them. The employees are smart enough to spot these behaviors and resent them. On the other hand, the managers genuinely respect those they work with, are supportive and helpful, and are interested in working as a team. Self-inquiry and persistence can change even the former type of supervisor into the latter.
    B. Many supervisors all into the trap of viewing employees as "things" to be manipulated, or try to motivate them by using a carrot-and-stick approach. These methods do not motivate employees, who often recognize the behaviors and resent them. Supervisors can change these behaviors, however, by using self-inquiry and persistence. The best managers are supportive and helpful, and have genuine respect for those with whom they work. They are interested in working as a team with those they supervise. To them, the Golden Rule is not "he or she who has the gold makes the rules."
    C. Some supervisors see employees as "things" to be used or manipulated using a carrot-and-stick technique. These methods don't work. Employees often see through them and resent them. A supervisor who

wants to change may do so. The techniques of self-inquiry and persistence can be used to turn him or her into the type of supervisor who doesn't think the Golden Rule is "he or she who has the gold makes the rules." They may become like the best managers who treat those with whom they work with respect and give them help and support. These are the manager who know how to build a team.

D. Unfortunately, many supervisors act as if their employees are objects whose movements they can position at will. This mistaken belief has the same result as another popular motivational technique—the carrot-and-stick approach. Both attitudes can lead to the same result—resentment from those employees who recognize the behaviors for what they are. Supervisors who recognize these behaviors can change through the use of persistence and the use of self-inquiry. It's important to remember that the best managers respect their employees. They readily give necessary help and support and are interested in working as a team with those they supervise. To these managers, the Golden Rule is not "he or she who has the gold makes the rules."

5. I. The first half of the nineteenth century produced a group of pessimistic poets—Byron, De Musset, Heine, Pushkin, and Leopardi.
II. It also produced a group of pessimistic composers—Schubert, Chopin, Schumann, and even the later Beethoven.
III. Above all, in philosophy, there was the profoundly pessimistic philosopher, Schopenhauer.
IV. The Revolution was dead, the Bourbons were restored, the feudal barons were reclaiming their land, and progress everywhere was being suppressed, as the great age was over.
V. "I thank God," said Goethe, "that I am not young in so thoroughly finished a world."

   A. "I thank God," said Goethe, "that I am not young in so thoroughly finished a world." The Revolution was dead, the Bourbons were restored, the feudal barons were reclaiming their land, and progress everywhere was being suppressed. The first half of the nineteenth century produced a group of pessimistic poets: Byron, De Musset, Heine, Pushkin, and Leopardi. It also produced pessimistic composers: Schubert, Chopin, Schumann. Although Beethoven came later, he fits into this group, too. Finally and above all, it also produced a profoundly pessimistic philosopher, Schopenhauer. The great age was over.

   B. The first half of the nineteenth century produced a group of pessimistic poets: Byron, De Musset, Heine, Pushkin, and Leopardi. It produced a group of pessimistic composers: Schubert, Chopin, Schumann, and even the later Beethoven. Above all, it produced a profoundly pessimistic philosopher, Schopenhauer. For each of these men, the great age was over. The Revolution was dead, and the Bourbons were restored. The feudal barons were reclaiming their land, and progress everywhere was being suppressed.

5._____

C. The great age was over. The Revolution was dead—the Bourbons were restored, and the feudal barons were reclaiming their land. Progress everywhere was being suppressed. Out of this climate came a profound pessimism. Poets, like Byron, De Musset, Heine, Pushkin, and Leopardi; composers, like Schubert, Chopin, Schumann, and even the later Beethoven; and above all, a profoundly pessimistic philosopher, Schopenauer. This pessimism which arose in the first half of the nineteenth century is illustrated by these words of Goethe, "I thank God that I am not young in so thoroughly finished a world."

D. The first half of the nineteenth century produced a group of pessimistic poets, Byron, De Musset, Heine, Pushkin, and Leopardi—and a group of pessimistic composers, Schubert, Chopin, Schumann, and the later Beethoven. Above it all, it produced a profoundly pessimistic philosopher, Schopenhauer. The great age was over. The Revolution was dead, the Bourbons were restored, the feudal barons were reclaiming their land, and progress everywhere was being suppressed. "I thank God," said Goethe, "that I am not young in so thoroughly finished a world."

6. I. A new manager sometimes may feel insecure about his or her competence in the new position.
   II. The new manager may then exhibit defensive or arrogant behavior towards those one supervises, or the new manager may direct overly flattering behavior toward one's new supervisor.

6._____

A. Sometimes, a new manager may feel insecure about his or her ability to perform well in this new position. The insecurity may lead him or her to treat others differently. He or she may display arrogant or defensive behavior towards those he or she supervises, or be overly flattering to his or her new supervisor.
B. A new manager may sometimes feel insecure about his or her ability to perform well in the new position. He or she may then become arrogant, defensive, or overly flattering towards those he or she works with.
C. There are times when a new manager may be insecure about how well he or she can perform in the new job. The new manager may also behave defensive or act in an arrogant way towards those he or she supervises, or overly flatter his or her boss.
D. Sometimes a new manager may feel insecure about his or her ability to perform well in the new position. He or she may then display arrogant or defensive behavior towards those they supervise, or become overly flattering towards their supervisors.

7. I. It is possible to eliminate unwanted behavior by bringing it under stimulus control—tying the behavior to a cue, and then never, or rarely, giving the cue.
   II. One trainer successfully used this method to keep an energetic young porpoise from coming out of her tank whenever she felt like it, which was potentially dangerous.
   III. Her trainer taught her to do it for a reward, in response to a hand signal, and then rarely gave the signal.

7._____

A. Unwanted behavior can be eliminated by tying the behavior to a cue, and then never, or rarely, giving the cue. This is called stimulus control. One trainer was able to use this method to keep an energetic young porpoise from coming out of her tank by teaching her to come out for a reward in response to a hand signal, and then rarely giving the signal.
B. Stimulus control can be used to eliminate unwanted behavior. In this method, behavior is tied to a cue, and then the cue is rarely, if ever, given. One trainer was able to successfully use stimulus control to keep an energetic young porpoise from coming out of her tank whenever she felt like it—a potentially dangerous practice. She taught the porpoise to come out for a reward when she gave a hand signal, and then rarely gave the signal.
C. It is possible to eliminate behavior that is undesirable by bringing it under stimulus control by tying behavior to a signal, and then rarely giving the signal. One trainer successfully used this method to keep an energetic porpoise from coming out of her tank, a potentially dangerous situation. Her trainer taught the porpoise to do it for a reward, in response to a hand signal, and then would rarely give the signal.
D. By using stimulus control, it is possible to eliminate unwanted behavior by tying the behavior to a cue, and then rarely or never give the cue. One trainer was able to use this method to successfully stop a young porpoise from coming out of her tank whenever she felt like it. To curb this potentially dangerous practice, the porpoise was taught by the trainer to come out of the tank for a reward, in response to a hand signal, and then rarely given the signal.

8.   I.   There is a great deal of concern over the safety of commercial trucks, caused by their greatly increased role in serious accidents since federal deregulation in 1981.
    II. Recently, 60 percent of trucks in New York and Connecticut and 70 percent of trucks in Maryland randomly stopped by state troopers failed safety inspections.
    III. Sixteen states in the United States require no training at all for truck drivers.

8.____

   A. Since federal deregulation in 1981, there has been a great deal of concern over the safety of commercial trucks, and their greatly increased role in serious accidents. Recently, 60 percent of trucks in New York and Connecticut, and 70 percent of trucks in Maryland failed safety inspections. Sixteen states in the United States require no training at all for truck drivers.
   B. There is a great deal of concern over the safety of commercial trucks since federal deregulation in 1981. Their role in serious accidents has greatly increased. Recently, 60 percent of trucks randomly stopped in Connecticut and New York and 70 percent in Maryland failed safety inspections conducted by state troopers. Sixteen states in the United States provide no training at all for truck drivers.
   C. Commercial trucks have a greatly increased role in serious accidents since federal deregulation in 1981. This has led to a great deal of concern.

Recently, 70 percent of trucks in Maryland and 60 percent of trucks in New York and Connecticut failed inspection of those that were randomly stopped by state troopers. Sixteen states in the United States require no training for all truck drivers.

D. Since federal deregulation in 1981, the role that commercial trucks have played in serious accidents has greatly increased, and this has led to a great deal of concern. Recently, 60 percent of trucks in New York and Connecticut, and 70 percent of trucks in Maryland randomly stopped by state troopers failed safety inspections. Sixteen states in the U.S. don't require any training for truck drivers.

9.
  I. No matter how much some people have, they still feel unsatisfied and want more, or want to keep what they have forever.
  II. One recent television documentary showed several people flying from New York to Paris for a one-day shopping spree to buy platinum earrings, because they were bored.
  III. In Brazil, some people were ordering coffins that cost a minimum of $45,000 and are equipping them with deluxe stereos, televisions, and other graveyard necessities.

9.____

A. Some people, despite having a great deal, still feel unsatisfied and want more, or think they can keep what they have forever. One recent documentary on television showed several people enroute from Paris to New York for a one day shopping spree to buy platinum earrings, because they were bored. Some people in Brazil are even ordering coffins equipped with such graveyard necessities as deluxe stereos and televisions. The price of the coffins start at $45,000.

B. No matter how much some people have, they may feel unsatisfied. This leads them to want more, or to want to keep what they have forever. Recently, a television documentary depicting several people flying from New York to Paris for a one day shopping spree to buy platinum earrings. They were bored. Some people in Brazil are ordering coffins that cost at least $45,000 and come equipped with deluxe televisions, stereos and other necessary graveyard items.

C. Some people will be dissatisfied no matter how much they have. They may want more, or they may want to keep what they have forever. One recent television documentary showed several people, motivated by boredom, jetting from New York to Paris for a one-day shopping spree to buy platinum earrings. In Brazil, some people are ordering coffins equipped with deluxe stereos, televisions and other graveyard necessities. The minimum price for these coffins—$45,000.

D. Some people are never satisfied. No matter how much they have they still want more, or think they can keep what they have forever. One television documentary recently showed several people flying from New York to Paris for the day to buy platinum earrings because they were bored. In Brazil, some people are ordering coffins that cost $45,000 and are equipped with deluxe stereos, televisions and other graveyard necessities.

9 (#2)

10.
I. A television signal or video signal has three parts.
II. Its parts are the black-and-white portion, the color portion, and the synchronizing (sync) pulses, which keep the picture stable.
III. Each video source, whether it's a camera or a video-cassette recorder contains its own generator of these synchronizing pulses to accompany the picture that it's sending in order to keep it steady and straight.
IV. In order to produce a clean recording, a video-cassette recorder must "lock-up" to the sync pulses that are part of the video it is trying to record, and this effort may be very noticeable if the device does not have gunlock.

10.____

A. There are three parts to a television or video signal: the black-and-white part, the color part, and the synchronizing (sync) pulses, which keep the picture stable. Whether it's a video-cassette recorder or a camera, each video source contains its own pulse that synchronizes and generates the picture it's sending in order to keep it straight and steady. A video-cassette recorder must "lock up" to the sync pulses that are part of the video it's trying to record. If the device doesn't have gunlock, this effort must be very noticeable.

B. A video signal or television is comprised of three parts: the black-and-white portion, the color portion, and the sync (synchronizing) pulses, which keep the picture stable. Whether it's a camera or a video-cassette recorder, each video source contains its own generator of these synchronizing pulses. These accompany the picture that it's sending in order to keep it straight and steady. A video-cassette recorder must "lock up" to the sync pulses that are part of the video it is trying to record in order to produce a clean recording. This effort may be very noticeable if the device does not have gunlock.

C. There are three parts to a television or video signal: the color portion, the black-and-white portion, and the sync (synchronizing pulses). These keep the picture stable. Each video source, whether it's a video-cassette recorder or a camera, generates these synchronizing pulses accompanying the picture it's sending in order to keep it straight and steady. If a clean recording is to be produced, a video-cassette recorder must store the sync pulses that are part of the video it is trying to record. This effort may not be noticeable if the device does not have gunlock.

D. A television signal or video signal has three parts: the black-and-white portion, the color portion, and the synchronizing (sync) pulses. It's the sync pulses which keep the picture stable, which accompany it and keep it steady and straight. Whether it's a camera or a video-cassette recorder, each video source contains its own generator of these synchronizing pulses. To produce a clean recording, a video-cassette recorder must "lock up" to the sync pulses that are part of the video it is trying to record. If the device does not have gunlock, this effort may be very noticeable.

KEY (CORRECT ANSWERS)

1. C
2. B
3. A
4. B
5. D
6. A
7. B
8. D
9. C
10. D

PREPARING WRITTEN MATERIAL
EXAMINATION SECTION
TEST 1

DIRECTIONS: Each short paragraph below is followed by four restatements or summaries of the information contained within it. Select the one that most completely and accurately restates the information given in the paragraph. *PRINT THE LETTER OF THE CORRECT ANSWER IN THE SPACE AT THE RIGHT.*

1. India's night jasmine, or hurshinghar, is different from most flowering plants, in that its flowers are closed during the day, and open after dark. The scientific reason for this is probably that the plant has avoided competing with other flowers for pollinating insects and birds, and relies instead on the service of nocturnal bats that are drawn to the flower's nectar. According to an old Indian legend, however, the flowers sprouted from the funeral ashes of a beautiful young girl who had fallen hopelessly in love with the sun.   1.____
    A. Despite the Indian legend that explains why the hurshinghar's flowers open at dusk, scientists believe it has to do with competition for available pollinators.
    B. The Indian hurshinghar's closure of its flowers during the day is due to a lack of available pollinators.
    C. The hurshinghar of India has evolved an unhealthy dependency on nocturnal bats.
    D. Like most myths, the Indian legend of the hurshinghar's night-flowering has been disproved by science.

2. Charles Lindbergh's trans-Atlantic flight from New York to Paris made him an international hero in 1927, but he lived nearly another fifty years, and by most accounts they weren't terribly happy ones. The two greatest tragedies of his life—the 1932 kidnapping and murder of his oldest son, and an unshakeable reputation as a Nazi sympathizer during World War II—he blamed squarely on the rabid media hounds who stalked his every move.   2.____
    A. Despite the fact that Charles Lindbergh had a hand in the two greatest tragedies of his life, he insisted on blaming the media for his problems.
    B. Charles Lindbergh lived a largely unhappy life after the glory of his 1927 trans-Atlantic flight, and he blamed his unhappiness on media attention
    C. Charles Lindbergh's later life was marked by despair and disillusionment.
    D. Because of the rabid media attention sparked by Charles Lindbergh's 1927 trans-Atlantic flight, he would later consider it the last happy event of his life

3. The United States, one of the world's youngest nations in the early twentieth century, had yet to spread its wings in terms of foreign affairs, preferring to remain isolated and opposed to meddling in the affairs of others. But the fact remained that as a young nation situated on the opposite side of the globe from Europe, Africa, and Asia, the United States had much work to do in   3.____

establishing relations with the rest of the world. So, too, as the European colonial powers continued to battle for influence in North and South America, did the United States come to believe that it was proper for them to keep these nations from encroaching into their sphere of influence.
- A. The roots of the Monroe Doctrine can be traced to the foreign policy shift of the United States during the early nineteenth century.
- B. In the early nineteenth century, the United States shifted its foreign policy to reflect a growing desire to actively protect its interests in the Western Hemisphere.
- C. In the early nineteenth century, the United States was too young and undeveloped to have devised much in the way of foreign policy.
- D. The United States adopted a more aggressive foreign policy in the early nineteenth century in order to become a diplomatic player on the world stage.

4. Hertha Ayrton, a nineteenth-century Englishwoman, pursued a career in science during a time when most women were not given the opportunity to go to college. Her series of successes led to her induction into the Institution of Electrical Engineers in 1899, when she was the first woman to receive this professional honor. Her most noted accomplishment was the research and invention of an anti-gas fan that the British War Office used in the trench warfare of World War I. 4.____
- A. The British Army's success in World War I can be partly attributed to Hertha Ayrton, a groundbreaking British scientist.
- B. Hertha Ayrton was the first woman to be inducted into the Institution of Electrical Engineers.
- C. The injustices of nineteenth-century England were no match for the brilliant mind of Hertha Ayrton.
- D. Hertha Ayrton defied the restrictions of her society by building a successful scientific career.

5. Scientists studying hyenas in Tanzania's Ngorongoro Crater have observed that hyena clans have evolved a system of territoriality that allows each clan a certain space to hunt within the 100-square-mile area. These territories are not marked by natural boundaries, but by droppings and excretions from the hyenas' scent glands. Usually, the hyenas take these boundary lines very seriously; some hyena clans have been observed abandoning their pursuit of certain prey after the prey has crossed into another territory, even though no members of the neighboring clan are anywhere in sight. 5.____
- A. The hyenas of Ngorongoro Crater illustrate that the best way to peacefully co-exist within a limited territory is to strictly delineate and defend territorial borders.
- B. While most territorial boundaries are marked using geographical features, the hyenas of Ngorongoro Crater have devised another method.
- C. The hyena clans of Ngorongoro Crater, in order to co-exist within a limited hunting territory, have developed a method of marking strict territorial boundaries.
- D. As with most species, the hyenas of Ngorongoro Crater have proven the age-old motto: "To the victor go the spoils."

3 (#1)

6. The flood control policy of the U.S. Army Corps of Engineers has long been an obvious feature of the American landscape—the Corps seeks to contain the nation's rivers with an enormous network of dams and levees, "channelizing" rivers into small, confined routes that will stay clear of settled flood—plains when rivers rise. As a command of the U.S. Army, the Corps seems to have long seen the nation's rivers as an enemy to be fought; one of the agency's early training films speaks of the Corps' "battle" with its adversary, Mother Nature.

6.____

   A. The dams and levees built by the U.S. Army Corps of Engineers have at least defeated their adversary, Mother Nature.
   B. The flood control policy of the U.S. Army Corps of Engineers has often reflected a military point of view, making the nation's rivers into enemies that must be defeated.
   C. When one realizes that the flood policy of the U.S. Army Corps of Engineers has always relied on a kind of military strategy, it is only possible to view the Corps' efforts as a failure.
   D. By damming and channelizing the nation's rivers, the U.S. Army Corps of Engineers have made America's flood plains safe for farming and development.

7. Frogs with extra legs or missing legs have been showing up with greater frequency over the past decade, and scientists have been baffled by the cause. Some researchers have concluded that pesticide runoff from farms is to blame; others say a common parasite, the trematode, is the culprit. Now, a new study suggests that both these factors in combination have disturbed normal development in many frogs, leading to the abnormalities.

7.____

   A. Despite several studies, scientists still have no idea what is causing the widespread incidence of deformities among aquatic frogs.
   B. In the debate over what is causing the increase in frog deformities, environmentalists tend to blame pesticide runoff, while others blame a common parasite, the trematode.
   C. A recent study suggests that both pesticide runoff and natural parasites have contributed to the increasing rate of deformities in frogs.
   D. Because of their aquatic habitat, frogs are among the most susceptible organisms to chemical ad environmental change, and this is illustrated by the increasing rate of physical deformities among frog populations.

8. The builders of the Egyptian pyramids, to insure that each massive structure was built on a completely flat surface, began by cutting a network of criss-crossing channels into the pyramid's mapped-out ground space and partly filling the channels with water. Because the channels were all interconnected, the water was distributed evenly throughout the channel system, and all the workers had to do to level their building surface was cut away any rock above the waterline.

8.____

   A. The modern carpenter's level uses a principle that was actually invented several centuries ago by the builders of the Egyptian pyramids.
   B. The discovery of the ancient Egyptians' sophisticated construction techniques is a quiet argument against the idea that they were built by slaves.

C. The use of water to insure that the pyramids were level mark the Egyptians as one of the most scientifically advanced of the ancient civilizations.
D. The builders of the Egyptian pyramids used a simple but ingenious method for ensuring a level building surface with interconnected channels of water

9. Thunderhead Mountain, a six-hundred-foot-high formation of granite in the Black Hills of South Dakota, is slowly undergoing a transformation that will not be finished for more than a century, when what remains of the mountain will have become the largest sculpture in the world. The statue, begun in 1947 by a Boston Sculptor named Henry Ziolkowski, is still being carved and blasted by his wife and children into the likeness of Crazy Horse, the legendary chief of the Sioux tribe of American natives. The enormity of the sculpture—the planned length of one of the figure's arms is 263 feet—is understandable, given the historical greatness of Crazy Horse.   9.____
    A. Only a hero as great as Crazy Horse could warrant a sculpture so large that it will take morae than a century to complete.
    B. In 1947, sculptor Henry Ziolkowski began work on what he imagined would be the largest sculpture in the world—even though he knew he would not live to see it completed.
    C. The huge Black Hills sculpture of the great Sioux chief Crazy Horse, still being carried out by the family of Henry Ziolkowski, will some day be the largest sculpture in the world.
    D. South Dakota's Thunderhead Mountain will soon be the site of the world's largest sculpture, a statue of the Sioux chief Crazy Horse.

10. Because they were some of the first explorers to venture into the western frontier of North America, the French were responsible for the naming of several native tribes. Some of these names were poorly conceived—the worst of which was perhaps Eskimo, the name for the natives of the far North, which translates roughly as "eaters of raw flesh." The name is incorrect; these people have always cooked their fish and game, and they now call themselves the Inuit, a native term that means "the people."   10.____
    A. The first to explore much of North America's western frontier were the French, and they usually gave improper or poorly-informed names to the native tribes.
    B. The Eskimos of North America have never eaten raw flesh, so it is curious that the French would give them a name that means "eaters of raw flesh."
    C. The Inuit have fought for many years to overcome the impression that they eat raw flesh.
    D. Like many native tribes, the Inuit were once incorrectly named by French explorers, but they have since corrected the mistake themselves.

11. Of the 30,000 species of spiders worldwide, only a handful are dangerous to human beings, but this doesn't prevent many people from having a powerful fear of all spiders, whether they are venomous or not. The leading scientific theory about arachnophobia, as this fear is known, is that far in our evolutionary past, some species of spider must have presented a serious enough threat to people that the sight of a star-shaped body or an eight-legged walk was coded into our genes as a danger signal.

11.____

   A. Scientists theorize that peoples' widespread fear of spiders can be traced to an ancient spider species that was dangerous enough to trigger this fearful reaction.
   B. The fear known as arachnophobia is triggered by the sight of a star-shaped body or an eight-legged walk.
   C. Because most spiders have a uniquely shaped body that triggers a human fear response, many humans are afflicted with the fear of spiders known as arachnophobia.
   D. Though only a few of the planet's 30,000 spider species are dangerous to people, many people have an unreasonable fear of them.

12. From the 1970s to the 1990s, the percentage of Americans living in the suburbs climbed from 37% to 47%. In the latter part of the 1990s, a movement emerged that questioned the good of such a population shift—or at least, the good of the speed and manner in which this suburban land was being developed. Often, people began to argue, the planning of such growth was flawed, resulting in a phenomenon that has become known as suburban "sprawl," or the growth of suburban orbits around cities at rates faster than infrastructures could support, and in ways that are damaging to the environment

12.____

   A. The term "urban sprawl" was coined in the 1990s, when the movement against unchecked suburban development began to gather momentum.
   B. In the 1980s and 1990s, home builders benefited from a boom in their most favored demographic segment, suburban new home buyers.
   C. Suburban development tends to suffer from poor planning, which can lead to a lower quality of life for residents
   D. The surge in suburban residences in the late twentieth century was criticized by many as "sprawl" that could not be supported by existing resources

13. Medicare, a $200 billion-a-year program, processes 1 billion claims annually, and in the year 2000, the computer system that handles these claims came under criticism. The General Accounting Office branded Medicare's financial management system as outdated and inadequate—one in a series of studies and reports warning that the program is plagued with duplication, overcharges, double billings, and confusion among users.

13.____

   A. The General Accounting Office's 2000 report proves that Medicare is bloated bureaucracy in need of substantial reform.
   B. Medicare's confusing computer network is an example of how the federal government often neglects the programs that mean the most to average American citizens.

C. In the year 2000, the General Accounting Office criticized Medicare's financial accounting network as inefficient and outdated.
D. Because it has to handle so many claims each year, Medicare's financial accounting system often produces redundancies and errors.

14. The earliest known writing materials were thin clay tablets, used in Mesopotamia more than 5,000 years ago. Although the tablets were cheap and easy to produce, they had two major disadvantages: they were difficult to store, and once the clay had dried and hardened, a person could not write on them. The ancient Egyptians later discovered a better writing material—the thin bark of the papyrus reed, a plant that grew near the mouth of the Nile River, which could be peeled into long strips, woven into a mat-like layer, pounded flat with heavy mallets, and then dried in the sun.   14.____
    A. The Egyptians, after centuries of frustration with clay writing tablets, were finally forced to invent a better writing surface.
    B. With the bark of the papyrus reed, ancient Egyptians made a writing material that overcame the disadvantages of clay tablets.
    C. The Egyptian invention of the papyrus scroll was necessitated in part by a relative lack of available clay.
    D. The word "paper" can be traced to the innovations of the Egyptians, who made the first paper-like writing material from the bark of papyrus plant.

15. In 1850, the German pianomaker Heinrich Steinweg and his family stepped off an immigrant ship in New York City, threw themselves into competition with dozens of other established craftsmen, and defeated them all by reinventing the instrument. The company they created commanded the market for nearly the next century and a half, while their competitors—some of the most acclaimed pianomakers in the business—faded into obscurity. And all the while, Steinway & Sons, through their sponsorship and encouragement of the world's most distinguished pianists, helped define the cultural life of the young United States.   15.____
    A. The Steinways capitalized on weak competition during the mid-nineteenth century to capture the American piano market.
    B. Because of their technical and cultural innovations, the Steinways had an advantage over other American pianomakers.
    C. Heinrich Steinweg founded the Steinway piano empire in 1850.
    D. From humble immigrant origins, the Steinway family rose to dominate both the pianomaking industry and American musical culture.

16. Feng Shui, the ancient Chinese science of studying the natural environment's effect on a person's well-being, has gained new popularity in the design and decoration of buildings. Although a complex area of study, a basic premise of Feng Shui is that each building creates a unique field of energy which affects the inhabitants of that building or home. In recent years, decorators and realtors have begun to offer services which include a diagnosis of a building's Feng Shui, or energy.   16.____
    A. Feng Shui, the Chinese science of balancing environmental energies, has been given more aesthetic quality by recent practitioners.

B. Generally, practitioners of Feng Shui work to create balance within a room, carefully arranging sharp and soft surfaces to create a positive environment that suits the room's primary purpose.
C. The idea behind the Chinese "science" of Feng Sui objects give off certain energies that affect a building's inhabitants has been a difficult one for most Westerners to accept, but it is gaining in popularity.
D. The ancient Chinese science of Feng Shui, which studies the balance of energies in a person's environment, has become popular among those who design and decorate buildings.

17. Because the harsh seasonal variations of the Kansas plains make survival difficult for most plant life, the area is dominated by tall, sturdy grasses. The only tree that has been able to survive and prosper throughout the wide expanse of prairie is the cottonwood, which can take root and grow in the most extreme climatic conditions. Sometimes a storm will shear off a living branch and carry it downstream, where it may snag along a sandbar and take root. 17.____
    A. Among the plant life of the Kansas plains, the only tree is the cottonwood.
    B. The only prosperous tree on the Kansas plains is the cottonwood, which can take root and grow in a wide range of conditions.
    C. Only the cottonwood, whose branches can grow after being broken off and washed down a river, is capable of surviving the climatic extremes of the Kansas plains.
    D. Because it is the most widespread and hardiest tree on the Kansas plains, the cottonwood had become a symbol of pioneer grit and fortitude.

18. In the twenty-first century, it's easy to see the automobile as the keystone of American popular culture. Subtract linen dusters, driving goggles, and women's *crepe de chine* veils from our history, and you've taken the Roaring out of the Twenties. Take away the ducktail haircuts, pegged pants, and upturned collars from the teen Car Cult of the Fifties, and the decade isn't nearly as Fabulous. Were the chromed and tailfinned muscle cars of the automobile' Golden Age modeled after us, or were we mimicking them? 18.____
    A. Ever since its invention, the automobile has shaped American culture.
    B. Many of the familiar names we give historical era, such as "Roaring Twenties" and "Fabulous Fifties," were given because of the predominance of the automobile.
    C. Americans' tastes in clothing have been determined primarily by the cars they drive.
    D. Teenagers have had a fascination for automobiles ever since the motorcar was first invented.

19. Since the 1960s, an important issue for Canada has been the status of minority French-speaking Canadians, especially in the province of Quebec, whose inhabitants make up 30% of the Canadian population and trace their ancestry back to a Canada that preceded British influence. In response to pressure from Quebec nationalists, the government in 1982 added a Charter of Rights to the constitution, restoring important rights that dated back to the time of aboriginal treaties. Separatism is still a prominent issue, though successive 19.____

referendums and constitutional inquiries have not resulted in any realistic progress toward Quebec's independence.
- A. Despite the fact that Quebec's inhabitants have their roots in Canada's original settlers, they have been constantly oppressed by the descendants of those who came later, the British.
- B. It seems unavoidable that Quebec's linguistic and cultural differences with the rest of Canada will some day lead to its secession.
- C. French-speaking Quebec's activism over the last several decades has led to concessions by the Canadian government, but it seems that Quebec will remain a part of the country for some time.
- D. The inhabitants of Quebec are an aboriginal culture that has been exploited by the Canadian government for years, but they are gradually winning back their rights.

20. For years, musicians and scientists have tried to discover what it is about an eighteenth-century Stradivarius violin—which may sell for more than $1 million on today's market—that gives it its unique sound. In 1977, American scientist Joseph Nagyvary discovered that the Stradivarius is made of a spruce wood that came from Venice, where timber was stored beneath the sea, and unlike the dry-seasoned wood from which other violins were made, this spruce contains microscopic holes which add resonance to the violin's sound. Nagyvary also found the varnish used on the Stradivarius to be equally unique, containing tiny mineral crystals that appear to have come from ground-up gemstones, which would filter out high-pitched tones and give the violin a smoother sound.   20.____
    - A. After carefully studying Stradivarius violins to discover the source of their unique sound, an American scientist discovered two qualities in the construction of them that set them apart from other instruments: the wood from which they were made, and the varnish used to coat the wood.
    - B. The two qualities that give the Stradivarius violin such a unique sound are the wood, which adds resonance, and the finish, which filters out high-pitched tones.
    - C. The Stradivarius violin, because of the unique wood and finish used in its construction, is widely regarded as the finest string instrument ever manufactured in the world.
    - D. A close study of the Stradivarius violin has revealed that the best wood for making violins is Venetian spruce, stored underwater.

21. People who watch the display of fireflies on a clear summer evening are actually witnessing a complex chemical reaction called "bioluminescence," which turns certain organisms into living light bulbs. Organisms that produce this light undergo a reaction in which oxygen combines with a chemical called lucerfin and an enzyme called luciferase. Depending on the organism, the light produced from this reaction can range from the light green of the firefly to the bright red spots of a railroad worm.   21.____
    - A. Although the function of most displays of bioluminescence is to attract mates, as is the case with fireflies, other species rely on bioluminescence for different purposes.

B. Bioluminescence, a phenomenon produced by several organisms, is the result of a chemical reaction that takes place within the body of the organism.
C. Of all the organisms in the world, only insects are capable of displaying bioluminescence.
D. Despite the fact that some organisms display bioluminescence, these reactions produce almost no heat, which is why the light they create is sometimes referred to as cold light.

22. The first of America's "log cabin" presidents, Andrew Jackson rose from humble backcountry origins to become a U.S. congressman and senator, a renowned military hero, and the seventh president of the United States. Among many Americans, especially those of the western frontier, he was acclaimed as a symbol of the "new" American: self-made, strong through closeness to nature, and endowed with a powerful moral courage.
    A. Andrew Jackson was the first American president to rise from modest origins.
    B. Because he was born poor, President Andrew Jackson was more popular among Americans of the western frontier.
    C. Andrew Jackson's humble background, along with his outstanding achievements, made him into a symbol of American strength and self-sufficiency.
    D. Andrew Jackson achieved success as a legislator, soldier, and president because he was born humbly and had to work for every honor he ever received.

22.____

23. In the past few decades, while much of the world's imagination has focused on the possibilities of outer space, some scientists have been exploring a different frontier—the ocean floor. Although ships have been sailing the oceans for centuries, only recently have scientists developed vehicles strong enough to sustain the pressure of deep-sea exploration and observation. These fiberglass vehicles, called submersibles, are usually just big enough to take two or three people to the deepest parts of the oceans' floors.
    A. Modern submersible vehicles, thanks to recent technological innovations, are now exploring underwater cliffs, crevices, and mountain ranges that were once unreachable.
    B. While most people tend to fantasize about exploring outer space, they should be turning toward a more accessible realm—the depths of the earth's oceans.
    C. Because of the necessarily small size of submersible vehicles, exploration of the deep ocean is not a widespread activity.
    D. Recent technological developments have helped scientists to turn their attention from deep space to the deep ocean.

23.____

24. The panda—a native of the remote mountainous regions of China—subsists almost entirely on the tender shoots of the bamboo plant. This restrictive diet has allowed the panda to evolve an anatomical structure that is completely different from that of other bears, whose paws are aligned for running, stabbing, and scratching. The panda's paw has an over-developed wrist bone that juts out below the other claws like a thumb, and the panda uses this "thumb" to grip bamboo shoots while it strips them of their leaves. 24.____
    A. The panda is the only bear-like animal that feeds on vegetation, and it has a kind of thumb to help it grip bamboo shoots.
    B. The panda's limited diet of bamboo has led it to evolve a thumb-like appendage for grasping bamboo shoots.
    C. The panda's thumb-like appendage is a factor that limits its diet to the shoots of the bamboo plant.
    D. Because bamboo shoots must be held tightly while eaten, the panda's thumb-like appendage ensure that it is the only bear-like animal that eats bamboo.

25. The stability and security of the Balkan region remains a primary concern for Greece in post-Cold War Europe, and Greece's active participation in peacekeeping and humanitarian operations in Georgia, Albania, and Bosnia are substantial examples of this commitment. Due to its geopolitical position, Greece believes it necessary to maintain, at least for now, a more nationalized defense force than other European nations. It is Greece's hope that the new spirit of integration and cooperation will help establish a common European foreign affairs and defense policy that might ease some of these regional tensions, and allow a greater level of Greek participation in NATO's integrated military structure. 25.____
    A. Greece's proximity to the unstable Balkan region has led it to keep a more nationalized military, though it hopes to become more involved in a common European defense force.
    B. The Balkan states present a greater threat to Greece than any other European nation, and Greece has adopted a highly nationalist military force as a result.
    C. Greece, the only Balkan state to belong to NATO, has an isolationist approach to defense, but hopes to achieve greater integration in the organization's combined forces.
    D. Greece's failure to become more militarily integrated with the rest of Europe can be attributed to the failure to establish a common European defense policy.

KEY (CORRECT ANSWERS)

1.	A	11.	A
2.	B	12.	D
3.	B	13.	C
4.	D	14.	B
5.	C	15.	D
6.	B	16.	D
7.	C	17.	B
8.	D	18.	A
9.	C	19.	C
10.	D	20.	A

21. B
22. C
23. D
24. B
25. A

PHILOSOPHY, PRINCIPLES, PRACTICES, AND TECHNICS
OF
SUPERVISION, ADMINISTRATION, MANAGEMENT, AND ORGANIZATION

TABLE OF CONTENTS

	Page
MEANING OF SUPERVISION	1
THE OLD AND THE NEW SUPERVISION	1
THE EIGHT (8) BASIC PRINCIPLES OF THE NEW SUPERVISION	1
I. Principle of Responsibility	1
II. Principle of Authority	2
III. Principle of Self-Growth	2
IV. Principle of Individual Worth	2
V. Principle of Creative Leadership	2
VI. Principle of Success and Failure	2
VII. Principle of Science	3
VIII. Principle of Cooperation	3
WHAT IS ADMINISTRATION?	3
I. Practices Commonly Classed as "Supervisory"	3
II. Practices Commonly Classed as "Administrative"	3
III. Practices Commonly Classed as Both "Supervisory" and "Administrative"	4
RESPONSIBILITIES OF THE SUPERVISOR	4
COMPETENCIES OF THE SUPERVISOR	4
THE PROFESSIONAL SUPERVISOR-EMPLOYEE RELATIONSHIP	4
MINI-TEXT IN SUPERVISION, ADMINISTRATION, MANAGEMENT, AND ORGANIZATION	5
I. Brief Highlights	5
A. Levels of Management	6
B. What the Supervisor Must Learn	6
C. A Definition of Supervision	6
D. Elements of the Team Concept	6
E. Principles of Organization	6
F. The Four Important Parts of Every Job	7
G. Principles of Delegation	7
H. Principles of Effective Communications	7
I. Principles of Work Improvement	7
J. Areas of Job Improvement	7
K. Seven Key Points in Making Improvements	8

	L.	Corrective Techniques for Job Improvement	8
	M.	A Planning Checklist	8
	N.	Five Characteristics of Good Directions	9
	O.	Types of Directions	9
	P.	Controls	9
	Q.	Orienting the New Employee	9
	R.	Checklist for Orienting New Employees	9
	S.	Principles of Learning	10
	T.	Causes of Poor Performance	10
	U.	Four Major Steps in On-the-Job Instructions	10
	V.	Employees Want Five Things	10
	W.	Some Don'ts in Regard to Praise	11
	X.	How to Gain Your Workers' Confidence	11
	Y.	Sources of Employee Problems	11
	Z.	The Supervisor's Key to Discipline	11
	AA.	Five Important Processes of Management	12
	BB.	When the Supervisor Fails to Plan	12
	CC.	Fourteen General Principles of Management	12
	DD.	Change	12

II. Brief Topical Summaries — 13

- A. Who/What is the Supervisor? — 13
- B. The Sociology of Work — 13
- C. Principles and Practices of Supervision — 14
- D. Dynamic Leadership — 14
- E. Processes for Solving Problems — 15
- F. Training for Results — 15
- G. Health, Safety, and Accident Prevention — 16
- H. Equal Employment Opportunity — 16
- I. Improving Communications — 16
- J. Self-Development — 17
- K. Teaching and Training — 17
  1. The Teaching Process — 17
     a. Preparation — 17
     b. Presentation — 18
     c. Summary — 18
     d. Application — 18
     e. Evaluation — 18
  2. Teaching Methods — 18
     a. Lecture — 18
     b. Discussion — 18
     c. Demonstration — 19
     d. Performance — 19
     e. Which Method to Use — 19

PHILOSOPHY, PRINCIPLES, PRACTICES, AND TECHNICS
OF
SUPERVISION, ADMINISTRATION, MANAGEMENT, AND ORGANIZATION

MEANING OF SUPERVISION

The extension of the democratic philosophy has been accompanied by an extension in the scope of supervision. Modern leaders and supervisors no longer think of supervision in the narrow sense of being confined chiefly to visiting employees, supplying materials, or rating the staff. They regard supervision as being intimately related to all the concerned agencies of society, they speak of the supervisor's function in terms of "growth," rather than the "improvement" of employees.

This modern concept of supervision may be defined as follows: Supervision is leadership and the development of leadership within groups which are cooperatively engaged in inspection, research, training, guidance, and evaluation.

THE OLD AND THE NEW SUPERVISION

TRADITIONAL
1. Inspection
2. Focused on the employee
3. Visitation
4. Random and haphazard
5. Imposed and authoritarian
6. One person usually

MODERN
1. Study and analysis
2. Focused on aims, materials, methods, supervisors, employees, environment
3. Demonstrations, intervisitation, workshops, directed reading, bulletins, etc.
4. Definitely organized and planned (scientific)
5. Cooperative and democratic
6. Many persons involved (creative)

THE EIGHT (8) BASIC PRINCIPLES OF THE NEW SUPERVISION

I. Principle of Responsibility
   Authority to act and responsibility for acting must be joined.
   A. If you give responsibility, give authority.
   B. Define employee duties clearly.
   C. Protect employees from criticism by others.
   D. Recognize the rights as well as obligations of employees.
   E. Achieve the aims of a democratic society insofar as it is possible within the area of your work.
   F. Establish a situation favorable to training and learning.
   G. Accept ultimate responsibility for everything done in your section, unit, office, division, department.
   H. Good administration and good supervision are inseparable.

II. Principle of Authority
The success of the supervisor is measured by the extent to which the power of authority is not used.
   A. Exercise simplicity and informality in supervision
   B. Use the simplest machinery of supervision
   C. If it is good for the organization as a whole, it is probably justified.
   D. Seldom be arbitrary or authoritative.
   E. Do not base your work on the power of position or of personality.
   F. Permit and encourage the free expression of opinions.

III. Principle of Self-Growth
The success of the supervisor is measured by the extent to which, and the speed with which, he is no longer needed.
   A. Base criticism on principles, not on specifics.
   B. Point out higher activities to employees.
   C. Train for self-thinking by employees to meet new situations.
   D. Stimulate initiative, self-reliance, and individual responsibility
   E. Concentrate on stimulating the growth of employees rather than on removing defects.

IV. Principle of Individual Worth
Respect for the individual is a paramount consideration in supervision.
   A. Be human and sympathetic in dealing with employees.
   B. Don't nag about things to be done.
   C. Recognize the individual differences among employees and seek opportunities to permit best expression of each personality.

V. Principle of Creative Leadership
The best supervision is that which is not apparent to the employee.
   A. Stimulate, don't drive employees to creative action.
   B. Emphasize doing good things.
   C. Encourage employees to do what they do best.
   D. Do not be too greatly concerned with details of subject or method.
   E. Do not be concerned exclusively with immediate problems and activities.
   F. Reveal higher activities and make them both desired and maximally possible.
   G. Determine procedures in the light of each situation but see that these are derived from a sound basic philosophy.
   H. Aid, inspire, and lead so as to liberate the creative spirit latent in all good employees.

VI. Principle of Success and Failure
There are no unsuccessful employees, only unsuccessful supervisors who have failed to give proper leadership.
   A. Adapt suggestions to the capacities, attitudes, and prejudices of employees.
   B. Be gradual, be progressive, be persistent.
   C. Help the employee find the general principle; have the employee apply his own problem to the general principle.
   D. Give adequate appreciation for good work and honest effort.
   E. Anticipate employee difficulties and help to prevent them.
   F. Encourage employees to do the desirable things they will do anyway.
   G. Judge your supervision by the results it secures.

VII. Principle of Science
Successful supervision is scientific, objective, and experimental. It is based on facts, not on prejudices.
   A. Be cumulative in results.
   B. Never divorce your suggestions from the goals of training.
   C. Don't be impatient of results.
   D. Keep all matters on a professional, not a personal, level.
   E. Do not be concerned exclusively with immediate problems and activities.
   F. Use objective means of determining achievement and rating where possible.

VIII. Principle of Cooperation
Supervision is a cooperative enterprise between supervisor and employee.
   A. Begin with conditions as they are.
   B. Ask opinions of all involved when formulating policies.
   C. Organization is as good as its weakest link.
   D. Let employees help to determine policies and department programs.
   E. Be approachable and accessible—physically and mentally.
   F. Develop pleasant social relationships.

WHAT IS ADMINISTRATION

Administration is concerned with providing the environment, the material facilities, and the operational procedures that will promote the maximum growth and development of supervisors and employees. (Organization is an aspect and a concomitant of administration.)

There is no sharp line of demarcation between supervision and administration; these functions are intimately interrelated and, often, overlapping. They are complementary activities.

I. Practices Commonly Classed as "Supervisory"
   A. Conducting employees' conferences
   B. Visiting sections, units, offices, divisions, departments
   C. Arranging for demonstrations
   D. Examining plans
   E. Suggesting professional reading
   F. Interpreting bulletins
   G. Recommending in-service training courses
   H. Encouraging experimentation
   I. Appraising employee morale
   J. Providing for intervisitation

II. Practices Commonly Classified as "Administrative"
   A. Management of the office
   B. Arrangement of schedules for extra duties
   C. Assignment of rooms or areas
   D. Distribution of supplies
   E. Keeping records and reports
   F. Care of audio-visual materials
   G. Keeping inventory records
   H. Checking record cards and books

I. Programming special activities
J. Checking on the attendance and punctuality of employees

III. Practices Commonly Classified as Both "Supervisory" and "Administrative"
A. Program construction
B. Testing or evaluating outcomes
C. Personnel accounting
D. Ordering instructional materials

RESPONSIBILITIES OF THE SUPERVISOR

A person employed in a supervisory capacity must constantly be able to improve his own efficiency and ability. He represent the employer to the employees and only continuous self-examination can make him a capable supervisor.

Leadership and training are the supervisor's responsibility. An efficient working unit is one in which the employees work with the supervisor. It is his job to bring out the best in his employees. He must always be relaxed, courteous, and calm in his association with his employees. Their feelings are important, and a harsh attitude does not develop the most efficient employees.

COMPETENCES OF THE SUPERVISOR

I. Complete knowledge of the duties and responsibilities of his position.
II. To be able to organize a job, plan ahead, and carry through.
III. To have self-confidence and initiative.
IV. To be able to handle the unexpected situation and make quick decisions.
V. To be able to properly train subordinates in the positions they are best suited for.
VI. To be able to keep good human relations among his subordinates.
VII. To be able to keep good human relations between his subordinates and himself and to earn their respect and trust.

THE PROFESSIONAL SUPERVISOR-EMPLOYEE RELATIONSHIP

There are two kinds of efficiency: one kind is only apparent and is produced in organizations through the exercise of mere discipline; this is but a simulation of the second, or true, efficiency which springs from spontaneous cooperation. If you are a manager, no matter how great or small your responsibility, it is your job, in the final analysis, to create and develop this involuntary cooperation among the people whom you supervise. For, no matter how powerful a combination of money, machines, and materials a company may have, this is a dead and sterile thing without a team of willing, thinking, and articulate people to guide it.

The following 21 points are presented as indicative of the exemplary basic relationship that should exist between supervisor and employee:

1. Each person wants to be liked and respected by his fellow employee and wants to be treated with consideration and respect by his superior.
2. The most competent employee will make an error. However, in a unit where good relations exist between the supervisor and his employees, tenseness and fear do not exist. Thus, errors are not hidden or covered up, and the efficiency of a unit is not impaired.

3. Subordinates resent rules, regulations, or orders that are unreasonable or unexplained.
4. Subordinates are quick to resent unfairness, harshness, injustices, and favoritism.
5. An employee will accept responsibility if he knows that he will be complimented for a job well done, and not too harshly chastised for failure; that his supervisor will check the cause of the failure, and, if it was the supervisor's fault, he will assume the blame therefore. If it was the employee's fault, his supervisor will explain the correct method or means of handling the responsibility.
6. An employee wants to receive credit for a suggestion he has made, that is used. If a suggestion cannot be used, the employee is entitled to an explanation. The supervisor should not say "no" and close the subject.
7. Fear and worry slow up a worker's ability. Poor working environment can impair his physical and mental health. A good supervisor avoids forceful methods, threats, and arguments to get a job done.
8. A forceful supervisor is able to train his employees individually and as a team, and is able to motivate them in the proper channels.
9. A mature supervisor is able to properly evaluate his subordinates and to keep them happy and satisfied.
10. A sensitive supervisor will never patronize his subordinates.
11. A worthy supervisor will respect his employees' confidences.
12. Definite and clear-cut responsibilities should be assigned to each executive.
13. Responsibility should always be coupled with corresponding authority.
14. No change should be made in the scope or responsibilities of a position without a definite understanding to that effect on the part of all persons concerned.
15. No executive or employee, occupying a single position in the organization, should be subject to definite orders from more than one source.
16. Orders should never be given to subordinates over the head of a responsible executive. Rather than do this, the officer in question should be supplanted.
17. Criticisms of subordinates should, whoever possible, be made privately, and in no case should a subordinate be criticized in the presence of executives or employees of equal or lower rank.
18. No dispute or difference between executives or employees as to authority or responsibilities should be considered too trivial for prompt and careful adjudication.
19. Promotions, wage changes, and disciplinary action should always be approved by the executive immediately superior to the one directly responsible.
20. No executive or employee should ever be required, or expected, to be at the same time an assistant to, and critic of, another.
21. Any executive whose work is subject to regular inspection should, wherever practicable, be given the assistance and facilities necessary to enable him to maintain an independent check of the quality of his work.

MINI-TEXT IN SUPERVISION, ADMINISTRATION, MANAGEMENT, AND ORGANIZATION

I. Brief Highlights

Listed concisely and sequentially are major headings and important data in the field for quick recall and review.

A. Levels of Management
Any organization of some size has several levels of management. In terms of a ladder, the levels are:

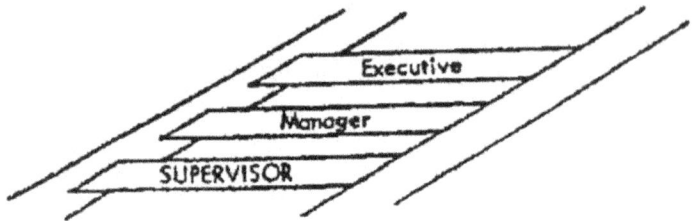

The first level is very important because it is the beginning point of management leadership.

B. What the Supervisor Must Learn
A supervisor must learn to:
1. Deal with people and their differences
2. Get the job done through people
3. Recognize the problems when they exist
4. Overcome obstacles to good performance
5. Evaluate the performance of people
6. Check his own performance in terms of accomplishment

C. A Definition of Supervisor
The term supervisor means any individual having authority, in the interests of the employer, to hire, transfer, suspend, lay-off, recall, promote, discharge, assign, reward, or discipline other employees or responsibility to direct them, or to adjust their grievances, or effectively to recommend such action, if, in connection with the foregoing, exercise of such authority is not of a merely routine or clerical nature but requires the use of independent judgment.

D. Elements of the Team Concept
What is involved in teamwork? The component parts are:
1. Members
2. A leader
3. Goals
4. Plans
5. Cooperation
6. Spirit

E. Principles of Organization
1. A team member must know what his job is.
2. Be sure that the nature and scope of a job are understood.
3. Authority and responsibility should be carefully spelled out.
4. A supervisor should be permitted to make the maximum number of decisions affecting his employees.
5. Employees should report to only one supervisor.
6. A supervisor should direct only as many employees as he can handle effectively.
7. An organization plan should be flexible.

8. Inspection and performance of work should be separate.
9. Organizational problems should receive immediate attention.
10. Assign work in line with ability and experience.

F. The Four Important Parts of Every Job
1. Inherent in every job is the *accountability* for results.
2. A second set of factors in every job is *responsibilities*.
3. Along with duties and responsibilities one must have the *authority* to act within certain limits without obtaining permission to proceed.
4. No job exists in a vacuum. The supervisor is surrounded by key *relationships*.

G. Principles of Delegation
Where work is delegated for the first time, the supervisor should think in terms of these questions:
1. Who is best qualified to do this?
2. Can an employee improve his abilities by doing this?
3. How long should an employee spend on this?
4. Are there any special problems for which he will need guidance?
5. How broad a delegation can I make?

H. Principles of Effective Communications
1. Determine the media.
2. To whom directed?
3. Identification and source authority.
4. Is communication understood?

I. Principles of Work Improvement
1. Most people usually do only the work which is assigned to them.
2. Workers are likely to fit assigned work into the time available to perform it.
3. A good workload usually stimulates output.
4. People usually do their best work when they know that results will be reviewed or inspected.
5. Employees usually feel that someone else is responsible for conditions of work, workplace layout, job methods, type of tools/equipment, and other such factors.
6. Employees are usually defensive about their job security.
7. Employees have natural resistance to change.
8. Employees can support or destroy a supervisor.
9. A supervisor usually earns the respect of his people through his personal example of diligence and efficiency.

J. Areas of Job Improvement
The areas of job improvement are quite numerous, but the most common ones which a supervisor can identify and utilize are:
1. Departmental layout
2. Flow of work
3. Workplace layout
4. Utilization of manpower
5. Work methods
6. Materials handling

8

       7. Utilization
       8. Motion economy

K. Seven Key Points in Making Improvements
       1. Select the job to be improved
       2. Study how it is being done now
       3. Question the present method
       4. Determine actions to be taken
       5. Chart proposed method
       6. Get approval and apply
       7. Solicit worker participation

l. Corrective Techniques of Job Improvement
Specific Problems
       1. Size of workload
       2. Inability to meet schedules
       3. Strain and fatigue
       4. Improper use of men and skills
       5. Waste, poor quality, unsafe conditions
       6. Bottleneck conditions that hinder output
       7. Poor utilization of equipment and machine
       8. Efficiency and productivity of labor

General Improvement
       1. Departmental layout
       2. Flow of work
       3. Work plan layout
       4. Utilization of manpower
       5. Work methods
       6. Materials handling
       7. Utilization of equipment
       8. Motion economy

Corrective Techniques
       1. Study with scale model
       2. Flow chart study
       3. Motion analysis
       4. Comparison of units produced to standard allowance
       5. Methods analysis
       6. Flow chart and equipment study
       7. Down time vs. running time
       8. Motion analysis

M. A Planning Checklist
       1. Objectives
       2. Controls
       3. Delegations
       4. Communications
       5. Resources
       6. Manpower

7. Equipment
8. Supplies and materials
9. Utilization of time
10. Safety
11. Money
12. Work
13. Timing of improvements

N. Five Characteristics of Good Directions
In order to get results, directions must be:
1. Possible of accomplishment
2. Agreeable with worker interests
3. Related to mission
4. Planned and complete
5. Unmistakably clear

O. Types of Directions
1. Demands or direct orders
2. Requests
3. Suggestion or implication
4. volunteering

P. Controls
A typical listing of the overall areas in which the supervisor should establish controls might be:
1. Manpower
2. Materials
3. Quality of work
4. Quantity of work
5. Time
6. Space
7. Money
8. Methods

Q. Orienting the New Employee
1. Prepare for him
2. Welcome the new employee
3. Orientation for the job
4. Follow-up

R. Checklist for Orienting New Employees   Yes   No
1. Do you appreciate the feelings of new employees
   when they first report for work?   ___   ___
2. Are you aware of the fact that the new employee must
   make a big adjustment to his job?   ___   ___
3. Have you given him good reasons for liking the job and
   the organization?   ___   ___
4. Have you prepared for his first day on the job? ___   ___
5. Did you welcome him cordially and make him feel needed? ___ ___

	Yes	No
6. Did you establish rapport with him so that he feels free to talk and discuss matters with you?	___	___
7. Did you explain his job to him and his relationship to you?	___	___
8. Does he know that his work will be evaluated periodically on a basis that is fair and objective?	___	___
9. Did you introduce him to his fellow workers in such a way that they are likely to accept him?	___	___
10. Does he know what employee benefits he will receive?	___	___
11. Does he understand the importance of being on the job and what to do if he must leave his duty station?	___	___
12. Has he been impressed with the importance of accident prevention and safe practice?	___	___
13. Does he generally know his way around the department?	___	___
14. Is he under the guidance of a sponsor who will teach the right way of doing things?	___	___
15. Do you plan to follow-up so that he will continue to adjust successfully to his job?	___	___

S. Principles of Learning
   1. Motivation
   2. Demonstration or explanation
   3. Practice

T. Causes of Poor Performance
   1. Improper training for job
   2. Wrong tools
   3. Inadequate directions
   4. Lack of supervisory follow-up
   5. Poor communications
   6. Lack of standards of performance
   7. Wrong work habits
   8. Low morale
   9. Other

U. Four Major Steps in On-The-Job Instruction
   1. Prepare the worker
   2. Present the operation
   3. Tryout performance
   4. Follow-up

V. Employees Want Five Things
   1. Security
   2. Opportunity
   3. Recognition
   4. Inclusion
   5. Expression

W. Some Don'ts in Regard to Praise
1. Don't praise a person for something he hasn't done.
2. Don't praise a person unless you can be sincere.
3. Don't be sparing in praise just because your superior withholds it from you.
4. Don't let too much time elapse between good performance and recognition of it

X. How to Gain Your Workers' Confidence
Methods of developing confidence include such things as:
1. Knowing the interests, habits, hobbies of employees
2. Admitting your own inadequacies
3. Sharing and telling of confidence in others
4. Supporting people when they are in trouble
5. Delegating matters that can be well handled
6. Being frank and straightforward about problems and working conditions
7. Encouraging others to bring their problems to you
8. Taking action on problems which impede worker progress

Y. Sources of Employee Problems
On-the-job causes might be such things as:
1. A feeling that favoritism is exercised in assignments
2. Assignment of overtime
3. An undue amount of supervision
4. Changing methods or systems
5. Stealing of ideas or trade secrets
6. Lack of interest in job
7. Threat of reduction in force
8. Ignorance or lack of communications
9. Poor equipment
10. Lack of knowing how supervisor feels toward employee
11. Shift assignments

Off-the-job problems might have to do with:
1. Health
2. Finances
3. Housing
4. Family

Z. The Supervisor's Key to Discipline
There are several key points about discipline which the supervisor should keep in mind:
1. Job discipline is one of the disciplines of life and is directed by the supervisor.
2. It is more important to correct an employee fault than to fix blame for it.
3. Employee performance is affected by problems both on the job and off.
4. Sudden or abrupt changes in behavior can be indications of important employee problems.
5. Problems should be dealt with as soon as possible after they are identified.
6. The attitude of the supervisor may have more to do with solving problems than the techniques of problem solving.
7. Correction of employee behavior should be resorted to only after the supervisor is sure that training or counseling will not be helpful.

12

8. Be sure to document your disciplinary actions.
9. Make sure that you are disciplining on the basis of facts rather than personal feelings.
10. Take each disciplinary step in order, being careful not to make snap judgments, or decisions based on impatience.

AA. Five Important Processes of Management
1. Planning
2. Organizing
3. Scheduling
4. Controlling
5. Motivating

BB. When the Supervisor Fails to Plan
1. Supervisor creates impression of not knowing his job
2. May lead to excessive overtime
3. Job runs itself—supervisor lacks control
4. Deadlines and appointments missed
5. Parts of the work go undone
6. Work interrupted by emergencies
7. Sets a bad example
8. Uneven workload creates peaks and valleys
9. Too much time on minor details at expense of more important tasks

CC. Fourteen General Principles of Management
1. Division of work
2. Authority and responsibility
3. Discipline
4. Unity of command
5. Unity of direction
6. Subordination of individual interest to general interest
7. Remuneration of personnel
8. Centralization
9. Scalar chain
10. Order
11. Equity
12. Stability of tenure of personnel
13. Initiative
14. Esprit de corps

DD. Change

Bringing about change is perhaps attempted more often, and yet less well understood, than anything else the supervisor does. How do people generally react to change? (People tend to resist change that is imposed upon them by other individuals or circumstances.

Change is characteristic of every situation. It is a part of every real endeavor where the efforts of people are concerned.

1. Why do people resist change?
   People may resist change because of:
   a. Fear of the unknown
   b. Implied criticism
   c. Unpleasant experiences in the past
   d. Fear of loss of status
   e. Threat to the ego
   f. Fear of loss of economic stability

2. How can we best overcome the resistance to change?
   In initiating change, take these steps:
   a. Get ready to sell
   b. Identify sources of help
   c. Anticipate objections
   d. Sell benefits
   e. Listen in depth
   f. Follow up

II. Brief Topical Summaries

   A. Who/What is the Supervisor?
      1. The supervisor is often called the "highest level employee and the lowest level manager."
      2. A supervisor is a member of both management and the work group. He acts as a bridge between the two.
      3. Most problems in supervision are in the area of human relations, or people problems.
      4. Employees expect: Respect, opportunity to learn and to advance, and a sense of belonging, and so forth.
      5. Supervisors are responsible for directing people and organizing work. Planning is of paramount importance.
      6. A position description is a set of duties and responsibilities inherent to a given position.
      7. It is important to keep the position description up-to-date and to provide each employee with his own copy.

   B. The Sociology of Work
      1. People are alike in many ways; however, each individual is unique.
      2. The supervisor is challenged in getting to know employee differences. Acquiring skills in evaluating individuals is an asset.
      3. Maintaining meaningful working relationships in the organization is of great importance.
      4. The supervisor has an obligation to help individuals to develop to their fullest potential.
      5. Job rotation on a planned basis helps to build versatility and to maintain interest and enthusiasm in work groups.
      6. Cross training (job rotation) provides backup skills.

7. The supervisor can help reduce tension by maintaining a sense of humor, providing guidance to employees, and by making reasonable and timely decisions. Employees respond favorably to working under reasonably predictable circumstances.
8. Change is characteristic of all managerial behavior. The supervisor must adjust to changes in procedures, new methods, technological changes, and to a number of new and sometimes challenging situations.
9. To overcome the natural tendency for people to resist change, the supervisor should become more skillful in initiating change.

C. Principles and Practices of Supervision
1. Employees should be required to answer to only one superior.
2. A supervisor can effectively direct only a limited number of employees, depending upon the complexity, variety, and proximity of the jobs involved.
3. The organizational chart presents the organization in graphic form. It reflects lines of authority and responsibility as well as interrelationships of units within the organization.
4. Distribution of work can be improved through an analysis using the "Work Distribution Chart."
5. The "Work Distribution Chart" reflects the division of work within a unit in understandable form.
6. When related tasks are given to an employee, he has a better chance of increasing his skills through training.
7. The individual who is given the responsibility for tasks must also be given the appropriate authority to insure adequate results.
8. The supervisor should delegate repetitive, routine work. Preparation of recurring reports, maintaining leave and attendance records are some examples.
9. Good discipline is essential to good task performance. Discipline is reflected in the actions of employees on the job in the absence of supervision.
10. Disciplinary action may have to be taken when the positive aspects of discipline have failed. Reprimand, warning, and suspension are examples of disciplinary action.
11. If a situation calls for a reprimand, be sure it is deserved and remember it is to be done in private.

D. Dynamic Leadership
1. A style is a personal method or manner of exerting influence.
2. Authoritarian leaders often see themselves as the source of power and authority.
3. The democratic leader often perceives the group as the source of authority and power.
4. Supervisors tend to do better when using the pattern of leadership that is most natural for them.
5. Social scientists suggest that the effective supervisor use the leadership style that best fits the problem or circumstances involved.
6. All four styles—telling, selling, consulting, joining—have their place. Using one does not preclude using the other at another time.

7. The theory X point of view assumes that the average person dislikes work, will avoid it whenever possible, and must be coerced to achieve organizational objectives.
8. The theory Y point of view assumes that the average person considers work to be a natural as play, and, when the individual is committed, he requires little supervision or direction to accomplish desired objectives.
9. The leader's basic assumptions concerning human behavior and human nature affect his actions, decisions, and other managerial practices.
10. Dissatisfaction among employees is often present, but difficult to isolate. The supervisor should seek to weaken dissatisfaction by keeping promises, being sincere and considerate, keeping employees informed, and so forth.
11. Constructive suggestions should be encouraged during the natural progress of the work.

E. Processes for Solving Problems
1. People find their daily tasks more meaningful and satisfying when they can improve them.
2. The causes of problems, or the key factors, are often hidden in the background. Ability to solve problems often involves the ability to isolate them from their backgrounds. There is some substance to the cliché that some persons "can't see the forest for the trees."
3. New procedures are often developed from old ones. Problems should be broken down into manageable parts. New ideas can be adapted from old one.
4. People think differently in problem-solving situations. Using a logical, patterned approach is often useful. One approach found to be useful includes these steps:
   a. Define the problem
   b. Establish objectives
   c. Get the facts
   d. Weigh and decide
   e. Take action
   f. Evaluate action

F. Training for Results
1. Participants respond best when they feel training is important to them.
2. The supervisor has responsibility for the training and development of those who report to him.
3. When training is delegated to others, great care must be exercised to insure the trainer has knowledge, aptitude, and interest for his work as a trainer.
4. Training (learning) of some type goes on continually. The most successful supervisor makes certain the learning contributes in a productive manner to operational goals.
5. New employees are particularly susceptible to training. Older employees facing new job situations require specific training, as well as having need for development and growth opportunities.
6. Training needs require continuous monitoring.
7. The training officer of an agency is a professional with a responsibility to assist supervisors in solving training problems.

8. Many of the self-development steps important to the supervisor's own growth are equally important to the development of peers and subordinates. Knowledge of these is important when the supervisor consults with others on development and growth opportunities.

G. Health, Safety, and Accident Prevention
1. Management-minded supervisors take appropriate measures to assist employees in maintaining health and in assuring safe practices in the work environment.
2. Effective safety training and practices help to avoid injury and accidents.
3. Safety should be a management goal. All infractions of safety which are observed should be corrected without exception.
4. Employees' safety attitude, training and instruction, provision of safe tools and equipment, supervision, and leadership are considered highly important factors which contribute to safety and which can be influenced directly by supervisors.
5. When accidents do occur, they should be investigated promptly for very important reasons, including the fact that information which is gained can be used to prevent accidents in the future.

H. Equal Employment Opportunity
1. The supervisor should endeavor to treat all employees fairly, without regard to religion, race, sex, or national origin.
2. Groups tend to reflect the attitude of the leader. Prejudice can be detected even in very subtle form. Supervisors must strive to create a feeling of mutual respect and confidence in every employee.
3. Complete utilization of all human resources is a national goal. Equitable consideration should be accorded women in the work force, minority-group members, the physically and mentally handicapped, and the older employee. The important question is: "Who can do the job?"
4. Training opportunities, recognition for performance, overtime assignments, promotional opportunities, and all other personnel actions are to be handled on an equitable basis.

I. Improving Communications
1. Communications is achieving understanding between the sender and the receiver of a message. It also means sharing information—the creation of understanding.
2. Communication is basic to all human activity. Words are means of conveying meanings; however, real meanings are in people.
3. There are very practical differences in the effectiveness of one-way, impersonal, and two-way communications. Words spoken face-to-face are better understood. Telephone conversations are effective, but lack the rapport of person-to-person exchanges. The whole person communicates.
4. Cooperation and communication in an organization go hand in hand. When there is a mutual respect between people, spelling out rules and procedures for communicating is unnecessary.
5. There are several barriers to effective communications. These include failure to listen with respect and understanding, lack of skill in feedback, and misinterpreting the meanings of words used by the speaker. It is also common

practice to listen to what we want to hear, and tune out things we do not want to hear.
6. Communication is management's chief problem. The supervisor should accept the challenge to communicate more effectively and to improve interagency and intra-agency communications.
7. The supervisor may often plan for and conduct meetings. The planning phase is critical and may determine the success or the failure of a meeting.
8. Speaking before groups usually requires extra effort. Stage fright may never disappear completely, but it can be controlled.

J. Self-Development
1. Every employee is responsible for his own self-development.
2. Toastmaster and toastmistress clubs offer opportunities to improve skills in oral communications.
3. Planning for one's own self-development is of vital importance. Supervisors know their own strengths and limitations better than anyone else.
4. Many opportunities are open to aid the supervisor in his developmental efforts, including job assignments; training opportunities, both governmental and non-governmental—to include universities and professional conferences and seminars.
5. Programmed instruction offers a means of studying at one's own rate.
6. Where difficulties may arise from a supervisor's being away from his work for training, he may participate in televised home study or correspondence courses to meet his self-development needs.

K. Teaching and Training
1. The Teaching Process
Teaching is encouraging and guiding the learning activities of students toward established goals. In most cases this process consists of five steps: preparation, presentation, summarization, evaluation, and application.

   a. Preparation
   Preparation is two-fold in nature; that of the supervisor and the employee. Preparation by the supervisor is absolutely essential to success. He must know what, when, where, how, and whom he will teach. Some of the factors that should be considered are:
   1) The objectives
   2) The materials needed
   3) The methods to be used
   4) Employee participation
   5) Employee interest
   6) Training aids
   7) Evaluation
   8) Summarization

   Employee preparation consists in preparing the employee to receive the material. Probably the most important single factor in the preparation of the employee is arousing and maintaining his interest. He must know the objectives of the training, why he is there, how the material can be used, and its importance to him.

b. Presentation
In presentation, have a carefully designed plan and follow it. The plan should be accurate and complete, yet flexible enough to meet situations as they arise. The method of presentation will be determined by the particular situation and objectives.

c. Summary
A summary should be made at the end of every training unit and program. In addition, there may be internal summaries depending on the nature of the material being taught. The important thing is that the trainee must always be able to understand how each part of the new material relates to the whole.

d. Application
The supervisor must arrange work so the employee will be given a chance to apply new knowledge or skills while the material is still clear in his mind and interest is high. The trainee does not really know whether he has learned the material until he has been given a chance to apply it. If the material is not applied, it loses most of its value.

e. Evaluation
The purpose of all training is to promote learning. To determine whether the training has been a success or failure, the supervisor must evaluate this learning.
In the broadest sense, evaluation includes all the devices, methods, skills, and techniques used by the supervisor to keep himself and the employees informed as to their progress toward the objectives they are pursuing. The extent to which the employee has mastered the knowledge, skills, and abilities, or changed his attitudes, as determined by the program objectives, is the extent to which instruction has succeeded or failed.
Evaluation should not be confined to the end of the lesson, day, or program but should be used continuously. We shall note later the way this relates to the rest of the teaching process.

2. Teaching Methods
A teaching method is a pattern of identifiable student and instructor activity used in presenting training material.
All supervisors are faced with the problem of deciding which method should be used at a given time.

a. Lecture
The lecture is direct oral presentation of material by the supervisor. The present trend is to place less emphasis on the trainer's activity and more on that of the trainee.

b. Discussion
Teaching by discussion or conference involves using questions and other techniques to arouse interest and focus attention upon certain areas, and by doing so creating a learning situation. This can be one of the most

valuable methods because it gives the employees an opportunity to express their ideas and pool their knowledge.

    c. Demonstration
The demonstration is used to teach how something works or how to do something. It can be used to show a principle or what the results of a series of actions will be. A well-staged demonstration is particularly effective because it shows proper methods of performance in a realistic manner.

    d. Performance
Performance is one of the most fundamental of all learning techniques or teaching methods. The trainee may be able to tell how a specific operation should be performed but he cannot be sure he knows how to perform the operation until he has done so.
As with all methods, there are certain advantages and disadvantages to each method.

    e. Which Method to Use
Moreover, there are other methods and techniques of teaching. It is difficult to use any method without other methods entering into it. In any learning situation, a combination of methods is usually more effective than any one method alone.

Finally, evaluation must be integrated into the other aspects of the teaching-learning process.

It must be used in the motivation of the trainees; it must be used to assist in developing understanding during the training; and it must be related to employee application of the results of training.

This is distinctly the role of the supervisor.